Bhagavad-Gita
&
Ten Principal Upanishads

Translated By
Purohit Swami

Alight Publications

2016

Bhagavad-Gita & Ten Principal Upanishads

By Purohit Swami

Published by Alight Publications in 2016

Alight Publications
PO Box 277
Live Oak, CA 95953

http://www.Alightbooks.com

Cover design © 2016 by Partap Singh. All rights reserved.

ISBN 1-931833-48-6

Printed in the United States of America

Dedicated
to the
Spiritual Pioneers
who have helped to
Illuminate the West

The Bhagavad Gita

Translation by
Shri Purohit Swami.

A NOTE ABOUT THE TRANSLATOR

Shri Purohit Swami was born into a religious and wealthy family in Badners, India, in 1882. He studied philosophy and law, received his LL.B. from Decan College, Poona, married and had three children. However, he did not practice law, and instead spent his entire life in spiritual devotion. He wrote in his native Marathi, in Hindi, Sanskrit and English – poems, songs, a play, a novel, a commentary on The Bhagavad Gita and an autobiography. He left India in 1930 at the suggestion of his Master to interpret the religious life of India for the West, and made his new home in England. It was here that he produced beautiful translations of The Bhagavad Gita, Patanjali's Aphorisms of Yoga and – in collaboration with his great friend, the Irish poet W.B. Yeats – The Ten Principal Upanishads. He died in 1946.

CONTENTS

ONE: THE DESPONDENCY OF ARJUNA /

TWO: THE PHILOSOPHY OF DISCRIMINATION /

THREE: KARMA-YOGA – THE PATH OF ACTION /

FOUR: DNYANA-YOGA – THE PATH OF WISDOM /

FIVE: THE RENUNCIATION OF ACTION /

SIX: SELF-CONTROL /

SEVEN: KNOWLEDGE AND EXPERIENCE /

EIGHT: LIFE EVERLASTING /

NINE: THE SCIENCE OF SCIENCES AND THE MYSTERY OF MYSTERIES /

TEN: THE DIVINE MANIFESTATIONS /

ELEVEN: THE COSMIC VISION /

TWELVE: BHAKTI-YOGA – THE PATH OF LOVE /

THIRTEEN: SPIRIT AND MATTER /

FOURTEEN: THE THREE QUALITIES /

FIFTEEN: THE LORD-GOD /

SIXTEEN: DIVINE AND DEMONIC CIVILIZATION /

SEVENTEEN: THE THREEFOLD FAITH /

EIGHTEEN: THE SPIRIT OF RENUNCIATION /

PREFACE

The Bhagavad Gita has long been recognized as one of the world's spiritual classics and a guide to all on the path of Truth. It is sometimes known as the Song of the Lord or the Gospel of the Lord Shri Krishna. According to Western scholarship, it was composed later than the Vedas and the Upanishads – probably between the fifth and second centuries before Christ. It is a fragment, part of the sixth book of the epic poem The Mahabaratha.

The Mahabaratha tells of the Pandavas, Prince Arjuna and his four brothers, growing up in north India at the court of their uncle, the blind King Dhritarashtra, after the death of their father, the previous ruler. There is always great rivalry between the Pandavas or sons of Pandu and the Kauravas, the one hundred sons of Dhritarashtra. Eventually the old king gives his nephews some land of their own but his eldest son, Duryodhana, defeats Yudhisthira, the eldest Pandava, by cheating at dice, and forces him and his brothers to surrender their land and go into exile for thirteen years. On their return, the old king is unable to persuade his son Duryodhana to restore their heritage and, in spite of efforts at reconciliation by Sanjaya, Dhritarashtra's charioteer; by Bheeshma, his great warrior; and even by the Lord Krishna himself, war cannot be averted. The rival hosts face each other on the field of Kurukshetra. It is at this point that The Bhagavad Gita begins. When Prince Arjuna surveys the battlefield, he is overwhelmed with sorrow at the futility of war. The teachings of The Bhagavad Gita are spoken by the divine Lord Krishna, who is acting as the prince's charioteer. Their dialog is given to posterity by Sanjaya who has been given the power to see and hear everything during the battle. When Krishna has finished speaking to Arjuna, the two armies engage. The battle lasts eighteen days and by the end of it nearly all of the warriors on both sides are dead save Krishna and the five sons of Pandu.

ONE: THE DESPONDENCY OF ARJUNA

The King Dhritarashtra asked: "O Sanjaya! What happened on the sacred battlefield of Kurukshetra, when my people gathered against the Pandavas?"

Sanjaya replied: "The Prince Duryodhana, when he saw the army of the Pandavas paraded, aproached his preceptor Guru Drona and spoke as follows:

Revered Father! Behold this mighty host of the Pandavas, paraded by the son of King Drupada, thy wise disciple.

In it are heroes and great bowmen; the equals in battle of Arjuna and Bheema, Yuyudhana, Virata and Drupada, great soldiers all;

Dhrishtaketu, Chekitan, the valiant King of Benares, Purujit, Kuntibhoja, Shaibya – a master over many;

Yudhamanyu, Uttamouja, Soubhadra and the sons of Droupadi, famous men.

Further, take note of all those captains who have ranged themselves on our side, O best of Spiritual Guides! The leaders of my army. I will name them for you.

You come first; then Bheeshma, Karna, Kripa, great soldiers; Ashwaththama, Vikarna and the son of Somadhatta;

And many others, all ready to die for my sake; all armed, all skilled in war.

Yet our army seems the weaker, though commanded by Bheeshma; their army seems the stronger, though commanded by Bheema.

Therefore in the rank and file, let stand firm in their posts, according to battalions; and all you generals about Bheeshma.

Then to enliven his spirits, the brave Grandfather Bheeshma, eldest of the Kuru-clan, blew his conch, till it sounded like a lion's roar.

And immediately all the conches and drums, the trumpets and horns, blared forth in tumultuous uproar.

Then seated in their spacious war chariot, yoked with white horses, Lord Shri Krishna and Arjuna sounded their divine shells.

Lord Shri Krishna blew his Panchajanya and Arjuna his Devadatta, brave Bheema his renowned shell, Poundra.

The King Dharmaraja, the son of Kunti, blew the Anantavijaya, Nakalu and Sahadeo, the Sugosh and Manipushpaka, respectively.

And the Maharaja of Benares, the great archer, Shikhandi, the great soldier, Dhrishtayumna, Virata and Satyaki, the invincible,

And O King! Drupada, the sons of Droupadi and Soubhadra, the great soldier, blew their conches.

The tumult rent the hearts of the sons of Dhritarashtra, and violently shook heaven and earth with its echo.

Then beholding the sons of Dhritarashtra, drawn up on the battlefield, ready to fight, Arjuna, whose flag bore the Hanuman,

Raising his bow, spoke this to the Lord Shri Krishna: O Infallible! Lord of the earth! Please draw up my chariot betwixt the two armies,

So that I may observe those who must fight on my side, those who must fight against me; And gaze over this array of soldiers, eager to please the sinful sons of Dhritarashtra."

Sanjaya said: "Having listened to the request of Arjuna, Lord Shri Krishna drew up His bright chariot exactly in the midst between the two armies,

Whither Bheeshma and Drona had led all the rulers of the earth, and spoke thus: O Arjuna! Behold these members of the family of Kuru assembled.

There Arjuna noticed fathers, grandfathers, uncles, cousins, sons, grandsons, teachers, friends; Fathers-in-law and benefactors, arrayed on both sides. Arjuna then gazed at all those kinsmen before him.

And his heart melted with pity and sadly he spoke: O my Lord! When I see all these, my own people, thirsting for battle,

My limbs fail me and my throat is parched, my body trembles and my hair stands on end. The bow Gandeeva slips from my hand, and my skin burns. I cannot keep quiet, for my mind is in tumult.

The omens are adverse; what good can come from the slaughter of my people on this battlefield?

Ah my Lord! I crave not for victory, nor for the kingdom, nor for any pleasure. What were a kingdom or happiness or life to me,

When those for whose sake I desire these things stand here about to sacrifice their property and their lives:

Teachers, fathers and grandfathers, sons and grandsons, uncles, father-in-law, brothers-in- law and other relatives.

I would not kill them, even for three worlds; why then for this poor earth? It matters not if I myself am killed.

My Lord! What happiness can come from the death of these sons of Dhritarashtra? We shall sin if we kill these desperate men.

We are worthy of a nobler feat than to slaughter our relatives – the sons of Dhritarashtra; for, my Lord, how can we be happy of we kill our kinsmen?

Although these men, blinded by greed, see no guilt in destroying their kin, or fighting against their friends,

Should not we, whose eyes are open, who consider it to be wrong to annihilate our house, turn away from so great a crime?

The destruction of our kindred means the destruction of the traditions of our ancient lineage, and when these are lost, irreligion will overrun our homes.

When irreligion spreads, the women of the house begin to stray; when they lose their purity, adulteration of the stock follows.

Promiscuity ruins both the family and those who defile it; while the souls of our ancestors droop, through lack of the funeral cakes and ablutions.

By the destruction of our lineage and the pollution of blood, ancient class traditions and family purity alike perish.

The wise say, my Lord, that they are forever lost, whose ancient traditions are lost. Alas, it is strange that we should be willing to kill our own countrymen and commit a great sin, in order to enjoy the pleasures of a kingdom.

If, on the contrary, the sons of Dhritarashtra, with weapons in their hand, should slay me, unarmed and unresisting, surely that would be better for my welfare!"

Sanjaya said: "Having spoken thus, in the midst of the armies, Arjuna sank on the seat of the chariot, casting way his bow and arrow; heartbroken with grief."

Thus, in the Holy Book the Bhagavad Gita, one of the Upanishads, in the Science of the Supreme Spirit, in the Art of Self-Knowledge, in the colloquy between the Divine Lord Shri Krishna and the Prince Arjuna, stands the first chapter, entitled: The Despondency of Arjuna.

TWO: THE PHILOSOPHY OF DISCRIMINATION

Sanjaya then told how the Lord Shri Krishna, seeing Arjuna overwhelmed with compassion, his eyes dimmed with flowing tears and full of despondency, consoled him:

The Lord said: My beloved friend! Why yield, just on the eve of battle, to this weakness which does no credit to those who call themselves Aryans, and only brings them infamy and bars against them the gates of heaven?

O Arjuna! Why give way to unmanliness? O thou who art the terror of thine enemies! Shake off such shameful effeminacy, make ready to act!

Arjuna argued: My Lord! How can I, when the battle rages, send an arrow through Bheeshma and Drona, who should receive my reverence?

Rather would I content myself with a beggar's crust that kill these teachers of mine, these precious noble souls! To slay these masters who are my benefactors would be to stain the sweetness of life's pleasures with their blood.

Nor can I say whether it were better that they conquer me or for me to conquer them, since I would no longer care to live if I killed these sons of Dhritarashtra, now preparing for fight.

My heart is oppressed with pity; and my mind confused as to what my duty is. Therefore, my Lord, tell me what is best for my spiritual welfare, for I am Thy disciple. Please direct me, I pray.

For, should I attain the monarchy of the visible world, or over the invisible world, it would not drive away the anguish which is now paralyzing my senses.

Sanjaya continued: "Arjuna, the conqueror of all enemies, then told the Lord of All-Hearts that he would no fight, and became silent, O King!

Thereupon the Lord, with a gracious smile, addressed him who was so much depressed in the midst of the two armies.

Lord Shri Krishna said: Why grieve for those for whom no grief is due, and yet profess wisdom? The wise grieve neither for the dead nor the living.

There was never a time when I was not, nor thou, nor these princes were not; there will never be a time when we shall cease to be.

As the soul experiences in this body infancy, youth and old age, so finally it passes into another. The wise have no delusion about this.

Those external relations which bring cold and heat, pain and happiness, they come and go; they are not permanent. Endure them bravely, O Prince!

The hero whose soul is unmoved by circumstance, who accepts pleasure and pain with equanimity, only he is fit for immortality.

That which is not, shall never be; that which is, shall never cease to be. To the wise, these truths are self-evident.

The Spirit, which pervades all that we see, is imperishable. Nothing can destroy the Spirit. The material bodies which this Eternal, Indestructible, Immeasurable Spirit inhabits are all finite.

Therefore fight, O Valiant Man!

He who thinks that the Spirit kills, and he who thinks of It as killed, are both ignorant. The Spirit kills not, nor is It killed.

It was not born; It will never die, nor once having been, can It cease to be. Unborn, Eternal, Ever-enduring, yet Most Ancient, the Spirit dies not when the body is dead.

He who knows the Spirit as Indestructible, Immortal, Unborn, Always-the-Same, how should he kill or cause to be killed?

As a man discards his threadbare robes and puts on new, so the Spirit throws off Its worn- out bodies and takes fresh ones.

Weapons cleave It not, fire burns It not, water drenches It not, and wind dries It not.

It is impenetrable; It can be neither drowned nor scorched nor dried. It is Eternal, All- pervading, Unchanging, Immovable and Most Ancient.

It is named the Unmanifest, the Unthinkable, the Immutable. Wherefore, knowing the Spirit as such, thou hast no cause to grieve.

Even if thou thinkest of It as constantly being born, constantly dying, even then, O Mighty Man, thou still hast no cause to grieve.

For death is as sure for that which is born, as birth is for that which is dead. Therefore grieve not for what is inevitable.

The end and the beginning of beings are unknown. We see only the intervening formations. Then what cause is there for grief?

One hears of the Spirit with surprise, another thinks It marvelous, the third listens without comprehending. Thus, though many are told about It, scarcely is there one who knows It.

Be not anxious about these armies. The Spirit in man is imperishable.

Thou must look at thy duty. Nothing can be more welcome to a soldier than a righteous war. Therefore to waver in this resolve is unworthy, O Arjuna!

Blessed are the soldiers who find their opportunity. This opportunity has opened for thee the gates of heaven.

Refuse to fight in this righteous cause, and thou wilt be a traitor, lost to fame, incurring only sin.

Men will talk forever of thy disgrace; and to the noble, dishonour is worse than death.

Great generals will think that thou hast fled from the battlefield through cowardice; though once honoured thou wilt seem despicable.

Thine enemies will spread scandal and mock at thy courage. Can anything be more humiliating?

If killed, thou shalt attain Heaven; if victorious, enjoy the kingdom of earth. Therefore arise, O Son of Kunti, and fight!

Look upon pleasure and pain, victory and defeat, with an equal eye. Make ready for the combat, and thou shalt commit no sin.

I have told thee the philosophy of Knowledge. Now listen and I will explain the philosophy of Action, by means of which, O

Arjuna, thou shalt break through the bondage of all action.

On this Path, endeavour is never wasted, nor can it ever be repressed. Even a very little of its practice protects one from great danger.

By its means, the straying intellect becomes steadied in the contemplation of one object only; whereas the minds of the irresolute stray into bypaths innumerable.

Only the ignorant speak in figurative language. It is they who extol the letter of the scriptures, saying, "There is nothing deeper than this."

Consulting only their own desires, they construct their own heaven, devising arduous and complex rites to secure their own pleasure and their own power; and the only result is rebirth.

While their minds are absorbed with ideas of power and personal enjoyment, they cannot concentrate their discrimination on one point.

The Vedic Scriptures tell of the three constituents of life – the Qualities. Rise above all of them, O Arjuna, above all the pairs of opposing sensations; be steady in truth, free from worldly anxieties and centered in the Self.

As a man can drink water from any side of a full tank, so the skilled theologian can wrest from any scripture that which will serve his purpose.

But thou hast only the right to work, but none to the fruit thereof. Let not then the fruit of thy action be thy motive; nor yet be thou enamored of inaction.

Perform all thy actions with mind concentrated on the Divine, renouncing attachment and looking upon success and failure with an equal eye. Spirituality implies equanimity.

Physical action is far inferior to an intellect concentrated on the Divine. Have recourse then to Pure Intelligence. It is only the petty-minded who work for reward.

When a man attains to Pure Reason, he renounces in this world the results of good and evil alike. Cling thou to Right Action. Spirituality is the real art of living.

The sages guided by Pure Intellect renounce the fruit of action; and, freed from the chains of rebirth, they reach the highest bliss.

When thy reason has crossed the entanglements of illusion, then shalt thou become indifferent both to the philosophies thou hast heard and to those thou mayest yet hear.

When the intellect, bewildered by the multiplicity of holy scripts, stands unperturbed in blissful contemplation of the Infinite, then hast thou attained Spirituality.

Arjuna asked: My Lord! How can we recognize the saint who has attained Pure Intellect, who has reached this state of Bliss, and whose mind is steady? how does he talk, how does he live, and how does he act?

Lord Shri Krishna replied: When a man has given up the desires of his heart and is satisfied with the Self alone, be sure that he has reached the highest state.

The sage, whose mind is unruffled in suffering, whose desire is not roused by enjoyment, who is without attachment, anger or fear – take him to be one who stands at that lofty level.

He who wherever he goes is attached to no person and to no place by ties of flesh; who accepts good and evil alike, neither welcoming the one nor shrinking from the other – take him to be one who is merged in the Infinite.

He who can withdraw his senses from the attraction of their objects, as the tortoise draws his limbs within its shell – take it that such a one has attained Perfection.

The objects of sense turn from him who is abstemious. Even the relish for them is lost in him who has seen the Truth.

O Arjuna! The mind of him, who is trying to conquer it, is forcibly carried away in spite of his efforts, by his tumultuous senses.

Restraining them all, let him meditate steadfastly on Me; for who thus conquers his senses achieves perfection.

When a man dwells on the objects of sense, he creates an attraction for them; attraction develops into desire, and desire breeds anger.

Anger induces delusion; delusion, loss of memory; through loss of memory, reason is shattered; and loss of reason leads to destruction.

But the self-controlled soul, who moves amongst sense objects, free from either attachment or repulsion, he wins eternal Peace.

Having attained Peace, he becomes free from misery; for when the mind gains peace, right discrimination follows.

Right discrimination is not for him who cannot concentrate. Without concentration, there cannot be meditation; he who cannot meditate must not expect peace; and without peace, how can anyone expect happiness?

As a ship at sea is tossed by the tempest, so the reason is carried away by the mind when preyed upon by straying senses.

Therefore, O Might-in-Arms, he who keeps his senses detached from their objects – take it that his reason is purified.

The saint is awake when the world sleeps, and he ignores that for which the world lives. He attains Peace, into whom desires flow as rivers into the ocean, which though brimming with water remains ever the same; not he whom desire carries away.

He attains Peace who, giving up desire, moves through the world without aspiration, possessing nothing which he can call his own, and free from pride.

O Arjuna! This is the state of the Self, the Supreme Spirit, to which if a man once attain, it shall never be taken from him. Even at the time of leaving the body, he will remain firmly enthroned there, and will become one with the Eternal.

Thus, in the Holy Book the Bhagavad Gita, one of the Upanishads, in the Science of the Supreme Spirit, in the Art of Self-Knowledge, in the colloquy between the Divine Lord Shri Krishna and the Prince Arjuna, stands the second chapter, entitled: The Philosophy of Discrimination.

THREE: KARMA-YOGA – THE PATH OF ACTION

Arjuna questioned: My Lord! If Wisdom is above action, why dost Thou advise me to engage in this terrible fight?

Thy language perplexes me and confuses my reason. Therefore please tell me the only way by which I may, without doubt, secure my spiritual welfare.

Lord Shri Krishna replied: In this world, as I have said, there is a twofold path, O Sinless One! There is the Path of Wisdom for those who meditate, and the Path of Action for those who work.

No man can attain freedom from activity by refraining from action; nor can he reach perfection by merely refusing to act.

He cannot even for a moment, remain really inactive, for the Qualities of Nature will compel him to act whether he will or no.

He who remains motionless, refusing to act, but all the while brooding over sensuous object, that deluded soul is simply a hypocrite.

But, O Arjuna! All honour to him whose mind controls his senses, for he is thereby beginning to practise Karma-Yoga, the Path of Right Action, keeping himself always unattached.

Do thy duty as prescribed, for action for duty's sake is superior to inaction. Even the maintenance of the body would be impossible if man remained inactive.

In this world people are fettered by action, unless it is performed as a sacrifice. Therefore, O Arjuna, let thy acts be done without attachment, as sacrifice only.

In the beginning, when God created all beings by the sacrifice of Himself, He said unto them: "Through sacrifice you can procreate, and it shall satisfy all your desires.

Worship the Powers of Nature thereby, and let them nourish you in return; thus supporting each other, you shall attain your highest welfare.

For, fed, on sacrifice, nature will give you all the enjoyment you can desire. But he who enjoys what she gives without returning is, indeed, a robber."

The sages who enjoy the food that remains after the sacrifice is made are freed from all sin;

but the selfish who spread their feast only for themselves feed on sin only.

All creatures are the product of food, food is the product of rain, rain comes by sacrifice, and sacrifice is the noblest form of action.

All action originates in the Supreme Spirit, which is Imperishable, and in sacrificial action the all-pervading Spirit is consciously present.

Thus he who does not help the revolving wheel of sacrifice, but instead leads a sinful life, rejoicing in the gratification of his senses, O Arjuna, he breathes in vain.

On the other hand, the soul who meditates on the Self is content to serve the Self and rests satisfied within the Self; there remains nothing more for him to accomplish.

He has nothing to gain by the performance or non-performance of action. His welfare depends not on any contribution that an earthly creature can make.

Therefore do thy duty perfectly, without care for the results, for he who does his duty disinterestedly attains the Supreme.

King Janaka and others attained perfection through action alone. Even for the sake of enlightening the world, it is thy duty to act;

For whatever a great man does, others imitate. People conform to the standard which he has set.

There is nothing in this universe, O Arjuna, that I am compelled to do, nor anything for Me to attain; yet I am persistently active.

For were I not to act without ceasing, O prince, people would be glad to do likewise. And if I were to refrain from action, the human race would be ruined; I should lead the world to chaos, and destruction would follow.

As the ignorant act, because of their fondness for action, so should the wise act without such attachment, fixing their eyes, O Arjuna, only on the welfare of the world.

But a wise man should not perturb the minds of the ignorant, who are attached to action; let him perform his own actions in the right spirit, with concentration on Me, thus inspiring all to do the same.

Action is the product of the Qualities inherent in Nature. It is only the ignorant man who, misled by personal egotism, says: 'I am the doer.'

But he, O Mighty One, who understands correctly the relation of the Qualities to action, is not attached to the act for he perceives that it is merely the action and reaction of the Qualities among themselves.

Those who do not understand the Qualities are interested in the act. Still, the wise man who knows the truth should not disturb the mind of him who does not.

Therefore, surrendering thy actions unto Me, thy thoughts concentrated on the Absolute, free from selfishness and without anticipation of reward, with mind devoid of excitement, begin thou to fight.

Those who always act in accordance with My precepts, firm in faith and without caviling, they too are freed from the bondage of action.

But they who ridicule My word and do not keep it, are ignorant, devoid of wisdom and blind. They seek but their own destruction.

Even the wise man acts in character with his nature; indeed, all creatures act according to their natures. What is the use of compulsion then?

The love and hate which are aroused by the objects of sense arise from Nature; do not yield to them. They only obstruct the path.

It is better to do thine own duty, however lacking in merit, than to do that of another, even though efficiently. It is better to die doing one's own duty, for to do the duty of another is fraught with danger.

Arjuna asked: My Lord! Tell me, what is it that drives a man to sin, even against his will and as if by compulsion?

Lord Shri Krishna: It is desire, it is aversion, born of passion. Desire consumes and corrupts everything. It is man's greatest enemy.

As fire is shrouded in smoke, a mirror by dust and a child by the womb, so is the universe enveloped in desire.

It is the wise man's constant enemy; it tarnishes the face of wisdom. It is as insatiable as a flame of fire.

It works through the senses, the mind and the reason; and with their help destroys wisdom and confounds the soul.

Therefore, O Arjuna, first control thy senses and then slay desire, for it is full of sin, and is the destroyer of knowledge and of wisdom.

It is said that the senses are powerful. But beyond the senses is the mind, beyond the mind is the intellect, and beyond and greater than intellect is He.

Thus, O Mighty-in-Arms, knowing Him to be beyond the intellect and, by His help, subduing thy personal egotism, kill thine enemy, Desire, extremely difficult though it be.

Thus, in the Holy Book the Bhagavad Gita, one of the Upanishads, in the Science of the Supreme Spirit, in the Art of Self-Knowledge, in the colloquy between the Divine Lord Shri Krishna and the Prince Arjuna, stands the third chapter entitled: Karma-Yoga or the Path of Action.

FOUR: DNYANA-YOGA – THE PATH OF WISDOM

Lord Shri Krishna said: This imperishable philosophy I taught to Viwaswana, the founder of the Sun dynasty, Viwaswana gave it to Manu the lawgiver, and Manu to King Ikshwaku!

The Divine Kings knew it, for it was their tradition. Then, after a long time, at last it was forgotten.

It is the same ancient Path that I have now revealed to thee, since thou are My devotee and My friend. It is the supreme Secret.

Arjuna asked: My Lord! Viwaswana was born before Thee; how then canst Thou have revealed it to him?

Lord Shri Krishna replied: I have been born again and again, from time to time; thou too, O Arjuna! My births are known to Me, but thou knowest not thine.

I have no beginning. Though I am imperishable, as well as Lord of all that exists, yet by My own will and power do I manifest

Myself.

Whenever spirituality decays and materialism is rampant, then, O Arjuna, I reincarnate Myself!

To protect the righteous, to destroy the wicked and to establish the kingdom of God, I am reborn from age to age.

He who realizes the divine truth concerning My birth and life is not born again; and when he leaves his body, he becomes one with Me.

Many have merged their existences in Mine, being freed from desire, fear and anger, filled always with Me and purified by the illuminating flame of self-abnegation.

Howsoever men try to worship Me, so do I welcome them. By whatever path they travel, it leads to Me at last.

Those who look for success, worship the Powers; and in this world their actions bear immediate fruit.

The four divisions of society (the wise, the soldier, the merchant, the labourer) were created by Me, according to the natural distribution of Qualities and instincts. I am the author of them, though I Myself do no action, and am changeless.

My actions do not fetter Me, nor do I desire anything that they can bring. He who thus realizes Me is not enslaved by action.

In the light of wisdom, our ancestors, who sought deliverance, performed their acts. Act thou also, as did our fathers of old.

What is action and what is inaction? It is a question which has bewildered the wise. But I will declare unto thee the philosophy of action, and knowing it, thou shalt be free from evil.

It is necessary to consider what is right action, what is wrong action, and what is inaction, for mysterious is the law of action.

He who can see inaction in action, and action in inaction, is the wisest among men. He is a saint, even though he still acts.

The wise call him a sage, for whatever he undertakes is free from the motive of desire, and his deeds are purified by the fire of Wisdom.

Having surrendered all claim to the results of his actions, always contented and independent, in reality he does nothing, even though he is apparently acting.

Expecting nothing, his mind and personality controlled, without greed, doing bodily actions only; though he acts, yet he remains untainted.

Content with what comes to him without effort of his own, mounting above the pairs of opposites, free from envy, his mind balanced both in success and failure; though he acts, yet the consequences do not bind him.

He who is without attachment, free, his mind centered in wisdom, his actions, being done as a sacrifice, leave no trace behind.

For him, the sacrifice itself is the Spirit; the Spirit and the oblation are one; it is the Spirit Itself which is sacrificed in Its own fire, and the man even in action is united with God, since while performing his act, his mind never ceases to be fixed on Him.

Some sages sacrifice to the Powers; others offer themselves on the alter of the Eternal. Some sacrifice their physical senses in the fire of self-control; others offer up their contact with external objects in the sacrificial fire of their senses.

Others again sacrifice their activities and their vitality in the Spiritual fire of self- abnegation, kindled by wisdom.

And yet others offer as their sacrifice wealth, austerities and meditation. Monks wedded to their vows renounce their scriptural learning and even their spiritual powers.

There are some who practice control of the Vital Energy and govern the subtle forces of Prana and Apana, thereby sacrificing their Prana unto Apana, or their Apana unto Prana.

Others, controlling their diet, sacrifice their worldly life to the spiritual fire. All understand the principal of sacrifice, and by its means their sins are washed away.

Tasting the nectar of immortality, as the reward of sacrifice, they reach the Eternal. This world is not for those who refuse to sacrifice; much less the other world.

In this way other sacrifices too may be undergone for the Spirit's sake. Know thou that they all depend on action. Knowing this, thou shalt be free.

The sacrifice of wisdom is superior to any material sacrifice, for, O Arjuna, the climax of action is always Realisation.

This shalt thou learn by prostrating thyself at the Master's feet, by questioning Him and by serving Him. The wise who have realized the Truth will teach thee wisdom.

Having known That, thou shalt never again be confounded; and, O Arjuna, by the power of that wisdom, thou shalt see all these people as if they were thine own Self, and therefore as Me.

Be thou the greatest of sinners, yet thou shalt cross over all sin by the ferryboat of wisdom. As the kindled fire consumes the fuel, so, O Arjuna, in the flame of wisdom the embers of action are burnt to ashes.

There is nothing in the world so purifying as wisdom; and he who is a perfect saint finds that at last in his own Self.

He who is full of faith attains wisdom, and he too who can control his senses, having attained that wisdom, he shall ere long attain Supreme Peace.

But the ignorant man, and he who has no faith, and the sceptic are lost. Neither in this world nor elsewhere is there any happiness in store for him who always doubts.

But the man who has renounced his action for meditation, who has cleft his doubt in twain by the sword of wisdom, who remains always enthroned in his Self, is not bound by his acts.

Therefore, cleaving asunder with the sword of wisdom the doubts of the heart, which thine own ignorance has engendered, follow the Path of Wisdom and arise!

Thus, in the Holy Book the Bhagavad Gita, one of the Upanishads, in the Science of the Supreme Spirit, in the Art of Self-Knowledge, in the colloquy between the Divine Lord Shri Krishna and the Prince Arjuna, stands the fourth chapter entitled: Dnyana-Yoga or the Path of Wisdom.

FIVE: THE RENUNCIATION OF ACTION

Arjuna said: My Lord! At one moment Thou praisest renunciation of action; at another, right action. Tell me truly, I pray, which of these is the more conducive to my highest welfare?

Lord Shri Krishna replied: Renunciation of action and the path of right action both lead to the highest; of the two, right action is the better.

He is a true ascetic who never desires or dislikes, who is uninfluenced by the opposites and is easily freed from bondage.

Only the unenlightened speak of wisdom and right action as separate, not the wise. If any man knows one, he enjoys the fruit of both.

The level which is reached by wisdom is attained through right action as well. He who perceives that the two are one, knows the truth.

Without concentration, O Mighty Man, renunciation is difficult. But the sage who is always meditating on the Divine, before long shall attain the Absolute.

He who is spiritual, who is pure, who has overcome his senses and his personal self, who has realized his highest Self as the Self of all, such a one, even though he acts, is not bound by his acts.

Though the saint sees, hears, touches, smells, eats, moves, sleeps and breathes, yet he knows the Truth, and he knows that it is not he who acts.

Though he talks, though he gives and receives, though he opens his eyes and shuts them, he still knows that his senses are merely disporting themselves among the objects of perception.

He who dedicates his actions to the Spirit, without any personal attachment to them, he is no more tainted by sin than the water lily is wetted by water.

The sage performs his action dispassionately, using his body, mind and intellect, and even his senses, always as a means of purification.

Having abandoned the fruit of action, he wins eternal peace. Others unacquainted with spirituality, led by desire and clinging to the benefit which they think will follow their actions, become entangled in them.

Mentally renouncing all actions, the self-controlled soul enjoys bliss in this body, the city of the nine gates, neither doing anything himself nor causing anything to be done.

The Lord of this universe has not ordained activity, or any incentive thereto, or any relation between an act and its consequences. All this is the work of Nature.

The Lord does not accept responsibility for any man's sin or merit. Men are deluded because in them wisdom is submerged in ignorance.

Surely wisdom is like the sun, revealing the supreme truth to those whose ignorance is dispelled by the wisdom of the Self.

Meditating on the Divine, having faith in the Divine, concentrating on the Divine and losing themselves in the Divine, their sins dissolved in wisdom, they go whence there is no return.

Sages look equally upon all, whether he be a minister of learning and humility, or an infidel, or whether it be a cow, an elephant or a dog.

Even in this world they conquer their earth-life whose minds, fixed on the Supreme, remain always balanced; for the Supreme has neither blemish nor bias.

He who knows and lives in the Absolute remains unmoved and unperturbed; he is not elated by pleasure or depressed by pain.

He finds happiness in his own Self, and enjoys eternal bliss, whose heart does not yearn for the contacts of earth and whose Self is one with the Everlasting.

The joys that spring from external associations bring pain; they have their beginning and their endings. The wise man does not rejoice in them.

He who, before he leaves his body, learns to surmount the promptings of desire and anger is a saint and is happy.

He who is happy within his Self and has found Its peace, and in whom the inner light shines, that sage attains Eternal Bliss and becomes the Spirit Itself.

Sages whose sins have been washed away, whose sense of separateness has vanished, who have subdued themselves, and seek only the welfare of all, come to the Eternal Spirit.

Saints who know their Selves, who control their minds, and feel neither desire nor anger, find Eternal Bliss everywhere.

Excluding external objects, his gaze fixed between the eyebrows, the inward and outward breathings passing equally through his nostrils;

Governing sense, mind and intellect, intent on liberation, free from desire, fear and anger, the sage is forever free.

Knowing me as Him who gladly receives all offerings of austerity and sacrifice, as the Might Ruler of all the Worlds and the Friend of all beings, he passes to Eternal Peace.

Thus, in the Holy Book the Bhagavad Gita, one of the Upanishads, in the Science of the Supreme Spirit, in the Art of Self-Knowledge, in the colloquy between the Divine Lord Shri Krishna and the Prince Arjuna, stands the fifth chapter entitled: The Renunciation of Action.

SIX: SELF-CONTROL

Lord Shri Krishna said: He who acts because it is his duty, not thinking of the consequences, is really spiritual and a true ascetic; and not he who merely observes rituals or who shuns all action.

O Arjuna! Renunciation is in fact what is called Right Action. No one can become spiritual who has not renounced all desire.

For the sage who seeks the heights of spiritual meditation, practice is the only method, and when he has attained them, he must maintain himself there by continual self-control.

When a man renounces even the thought of initiating action, when he is not interested in sense objects or any results which may flow from his acts, then in truth he understands spirituality.

Let him seek liberation by the help of his Highest Self, and let him never disgrace his own Self. For that Self is his only friend; yet it may also be his enemy.

To him who has conquered his lower nature by Its help, the Self is a friend, but to him who has not done so, It is an enemy.

The Self of him who is self-controlled, and has attained peace is equally unmoved by heat or cold, pleasure or pain, honour or dishonour.

He who desires nothing but wisdom and spiritual insight, who has conquered his senses and who looks with the same eye upon a lump of earth, a stone or fine gold, is a real saint.

He looks impartially on all – lover, friend or foe; indifferent or hostile; alien or relative; virtuous or sinful.

Let the student of spirituality try unceasingly to concentrate his mind; Let him live in seclusion, absolutely alone, with mind and personality controlled, free from desire and without possessions.

Having chosen a holy place, let him sit in a firm posture on a seat, neither too high nor too low, and covered with a grass mat, a deer skin and a cloth.

Seated thus, his mind concentrated, its functions controlled and his senses governed, let him practice meditation for the purification of his lower nature.

Let him hold body, head and neck erect, motionless and steady; let him look fixedly at the tip of his nose, turning neither to the right nor to the left.

With peace in his heart and nor fear, observing the vow of celibacy, with mind controlled and fixed on Me, let the student lose himself in contemplation of Me.

Thus keeping his mind always in communion with Me, and with his thoughts subdued, he shall attain that Peace which is mine and which will lead him to liberation at last.

Meditation is not for him who eats too much, not for him who eats not at all; not for him who is overmuch addicted to sleep, not for him who is always awake.

But for him who regulates his food and recreation, who is balanced in action, in sleep and in waking, it shall dispel all unhappiness.

When the mind, completely controlled, is centered in the Self, and free from all earthly desires, then is the man truly spiritual.

The wise man who has conquered his mind and is absorbed in the Self is as a lamp which does not flicker, since it stands sheltered from every wind.

There, where the whole nature is seen in the light of the Self, where the man abides within his Self and is satisfied there, its functions restrained by its union with the Divine, the mind finds rest.

When he enjoys the Bliss which passes sense, and which only the Pure Intellect can grasp, when he comes to rest within his own highest Self, never again will he stray from reality.

Finding That, he will realise that there is no possession so precious. And when once established here, no calamity can disturb him.

This inner severance from the affliction of misery is spirituality. It should be practised with determination and with a heart which refuses to be depressed.

Renouncing every desire which imagination can conceive, controlling the senses at every point by the power of mind;

Little by little, by the help of his reason controlled by fortitude, let him attain peace; and, fixing his mind on the Self, let him not think of any other thing.

When the volatile and wavering mind would wander, let him restrain it and bring it again to its allegiance to the Self.

Supreme Bliss is the lot of the sage, whose mind attains Peace, whose passions subside, who is without sin, and who becomes one with the Absolute.

Thus, free from sin, abiding always in the Eternal, the saint enjoys without effort the Bliss which flows from realization of the Infinite.

He who experiences the unity of life sees his own Self in all beings, and all beings in his own Self, and looks on everything with an impartial eye;

He who sees Me in everything and everything in Me, him shall I never forsake, nor shall he lose Me.

The sage who realizes the unity of life and who worships Me in all beings, lives in Me, whatever may be his lot.

O Arjuna! He is the perfect saint who, taught by the likeness within himself, sees the same Self everywhere, whether the outer form be pleasurable or painful.

Arjuna said: I do not see how I can attain this state of equanimity which Thou has revealed, owing to the restlessness of my mind.

My Lord! Verily, the mind is fickle and turbulent, obstinate and strong, yea extremely difficult as the wind to control.

Lord Shri Krishna replied: Doubtless, O Mighty One, the mind is fickle and exceedingly difficult to restrain, but, O Son of Kunti, with practice and renunciation it can be done.

It is not possible to attain Self-Realisation if a man does not know how to control himself; but for him who, striving by proper means, learns such control, it is possible.

Arjuna asked: He who fails to control himself, whose mind falls from spiritual contemplation, who attains not perfection but retains his faith, what of him, my Lord?

Having failed in both, my Lord, is he without hope, like a riven cloud having no support, lost on the spiritual road?

My Lord! Thou art worthy to solve this doubt once and for all; save Thyself there is no one competent to do so.

Lord Shri Krishna replied: My beloved child! There is no destruction for him, either in this world or in the next. No evil fate awaits him who treads the path of righteousness.

Having reached the worlds where the righteous dwell, and having remained there for many years, he who has slipped from the path of spirituality will be born again in the family of the pure, benevolent and prosperous.

Or, he may be born in the family of the wise sages, though a birth like this is, indeed, very difficult to obtain.

Then the experience acquired in his former life will revive, and with its help he will strive for perfection more eagerly than before.

Unconsciously he will return to the practices of his old life; so that he who tries to realize spiritual consciousness is certainly superior to one who only talks of it.

Then after many lives, the student of spirituality, who earnestly strives, and whose sins are absolved, attains perfection and reaches the Supreme.

The wise man is superior to the ascetic and to the scholar and to the man of action; therefore be thou a wise man, O Arjuna!

I look upon him as the best of mystics who, full of faith, worshippeth Me and abideth in Me.

Thus, in the Holy Book the Bhagavad Gita, one of the Upanishads, in the Science of the Supreme Spirit, in the Art of Self-Knowledge, in the colloquy between the Divine Lord Shri Krishna and the Prince Arjuna, stands the sixth chapter entitled: Self-Control.

SEVEN: KNOWLEDGE AND EXPERIENCE

Lord Shri Krishna said: Listen, O Arjuna! And I will tell thee how thou shalt know Me in my Full perfection, practicing meditation with thy mind devoted to Me, and having Me for thy refuge.

I will reveal to this knowledge unto thee, and how it may be realized; which, once accomplished, there remains nothing else worth having in this life.

Among thousands of men scarcely one strives for perfection, and even amongst those who gain occult powers, perchance but one knows me in truth.

Earth, water, fire, air, ether, mind, intellect and personality; this is the eightfold division of My Manifested Nature.

This is My inferior Nature; but distinct from this, O Valiant One, know thou that my Superior Nature is the very Life which sustains the universe.

It is the womb of all being; for I am He by Whom the worlds were created and shall be dissolved.

O Arjuna! There is nothing higher than Me; all is strung upon Me as rows of pearls upon a thread.

O Arjuna! I am the Fluidity in water, the Light in the sun and in the moon. I am the mystic syllable Om in the Vedic scriptures, the Sound in ether, the Virility in man.

I am the Fragrance of earth, the Brilliance of fire. I am the Life Force in all beings, and I am the Austerity of the ascetics.

Know, O Arjuna, that I am the eternal Seed of being; I am the Intelligence of the intelligent, the Splendor of the resplendent.

I am the Strength of the strong, of them who are free from attachment and desire; and, O Arjuna, I am the Desire for righteousness.

Whatever be the nature of their life, whether it be pure or passionate or ignorant, they are all derived from Me. They are in Me, but I am not in them.

The inhabitants of the world, misled by those natures which the Qualities have engendered, know not that I am higher than them all, and that I do not change.

Verily, this Divine Illusion of Phenomenon manifesting itself in the Qualities is difficult to surmount. Only they who devote themselves to Me and to Me alone can accomplish it.

The sinner, the ignorant, the vile, deprived of spiritual perception by the glamour of Illusion, and he who pursues a godless life – none of them shall find Me.

O Arjuna! The righteous who worship Me are grouped by stages: first, they who suffer, next they who desire knowledge, then they who thirst after truth, and lastly they who attain wisdom.

Of all of these, he who has gained wisdom, who meditates on Me without ceasing, devoting himself only to Me, he is the best; for by the wise man I am exceedingly beloved and the wise man, too, is beloved by Me.

Noble-minded are they all, but the wise man I hold as my own Self; for he, remaining always at peace with Me, makes me his final goal.

After many lives, at last the wise man realises Me as I am. A man so enlightened that he sees God everywhere is very difficult to find.

They in whom wisdom is obscured by one desire or the other,

worship the lesser Powers, practising many rites which vary according to their temperaments.

But whatever the form of worship, if the devotee has faith, then upon his faith in that worship do I set My own seal.

If he worships one form alone with real faith, then shall his desires be fulfilled through that only; for thus have I ordained.

The fruit that comes to men of limited insight is, after all, finite. They who worship the Lower Powers attain them; but those who worship Me come unto Me alone.

The ignorant think of Me, who am the Unmanifested Spirit, as if I were really in human form. They do not understand that My Superior Nature is changeless and most excellent.

I am not visible to all, for I am enveloped by the illusion of Phenomenon. This deluded world does not know Me as the Unborn and the Imperishable.

I know, O Arjuna, all beings in the past, the present and the future; but they do not know Me.

O brave Arjuna! Man lives in a fairy world, deceived by the glamour of opposite sensations, infatuated by desire and aversion.

But those who act righteously, in whom sin has been destroyed, who are free from the infatuation of the conflicting emotions, they worship Me with firm resolution.

Those who make Me their refuge, who strive for liberation from decay and Death, they realize the Supreme Spirit, which is their own real Self, and in which all action finds its consummation.

Those who see Me in the life of the world, in the universal sacrifice, and as pure Divinity, keeping their minds steady, they live in Me, even in the crucial hour of death.

Thus, in the Holy Book the Bhagavad Gita, one of the Upanishads, in the Science of the Supreme Spirit, in the Art of Self-Knowledge, in the Colloquy between the Divine Lord Shri Krishna and the Prince Arjuna, stand the seventh chapter, entitled: Knowledge and Experience.

EIGHT: LIFE EVERLASTING

Arjuna asked: O Lord of Lords! What is that which men call the Supreme Spirit, what is man's Spiritual Nature, and what is the Law? What is Matter and what is Divinity?

Who is it who rules the spirit sacrifice in many; and at the time of death how may those who have learned self-control come to the knowledge of Thee?

The Lord Shri Krishna replied: The Supreme Spirit is the Highest Imperishable Self, and Its Nature is spiritual consciousness. The worlds have been created and are supported by an emanation from the Spirit which is called the Law.

Matter consists of the forms that perish; Divinity is the Supreme Self; and He who inspires the spirit of sacrifice in man, O noblest of thy race, is I Myself, Who now stand in human form before thee.

Whosoever at the time of death thinks only of Me, and thinking thus leaves the body and goes forth, assuredly he will know Me.

On whatever sphere of being the mind of a man may be intent at the time of death, thither he will go.

Therefore meditate always on Me, and fight; if thy mind and thy reason be fixed on Me, to Me shalt thou surely come.

He whose mind does not wander, and who is engaged in constant meditation, attains the Supreme Spirit.

Whoso meditates on the Omniscient, the Ancient, more minute than the atom, yet the Ruler and Upholder of all, Unimaginable, Brilliant like the Sun, Beyond the reach of darkness;

He who leaves the body with mind unmoved and filled with devotion, by the power of his meditation gathering between his eyebrows his whole vital energy, attains the Supreme.

Now I will speak briefly of the imperishable goal, proclaimed by those versed in the scriptures, which the mystic attains when free from passion, and for which he is content to undergo the vow of continence.

Closing the gates of the body, drawing the forces of his mind into the heart and by the power of meditation concentrating his vital energy in the brain;

Repeating Om, the Symbol of Eternity, holding Me always in remembrance, he who thus leaves his body and goes forth reaches the Spirit Supreme.

To him who thinks constantly of Me, and of nothing else, to such an ever-faithful devotee, O Arjuna, am I ever accessible.

Coming thus unto Me, these great souls go no more to the misery and death of earthly life, for they have gained perfection.

The worlds, with the whole realm of creation, come and go; but, O Arjuna, whoso comes to Me, for him there is nor rebirth.

Those who understand the cosmic day and cosmic night know that one day of creation is a thousand cycles, and that the night is of equal length.

At the dawning of that day all objects in manifestation stream forth from the Unmanifest, and when evening falls they are dissolved into It again.

The same multitude of beings, which have lived on earth so often, all are dissolved as the night of the universe approaches, to issue forth anew when morning breaks. Thus is it ordained.

In truth, therefore, there is the Eternal Unmanifest, which is beyond and above the Unmanifest Spirit of Creation, which is never destroyed when all these being perish.

The wise say that the Unmanifest and Indestructible is the highest goal of all; when once That is reached, there is no return. That is My Blessed Home.

O Arjuna! That Highest God, in Whom all beings abide, and Who pervades the entire universe, is reached only by wholehearted devotion.

[The following material (between the asterisks) is an example of what may be a 'doctored' inclusion. It does not jibe with the rest of the material because it is not presented as metaphor and clearly implies that worldly phenomena are spiritually determining. Maybe it was added by an individual or individuals who were less cognizant than the originating author. Or maybe was 'craftily' inserted to function as a sort of litmus test – those who get 'taken in' by it may be recognized as not having 'spiritual discernment'.]

*Now I will tell thee, O Arjuna, of the times at which, if the mystics go forth, they do not return, and at which they go forth only to return.

If knowing the Supreme Spirit the sage goes forth with fire and light, in the daytime, in the fortnight of the waxing moon and in the six months before the Northern summer solstice, he will attain the Supreme.

But if he departs in gloom, at night, during the fortnight of the waning moon and in the six months before the Southern solstice, then he reaches but lunar light and he will be born again.

These bright and dark paths out of the world have always existed. Whoso takes the former, returns not; he who chooses the latter, returns.*

O Arjuna! The saint knowing these paths is not confused. Therefore meditate perpetually. The sage who knows this passes beyond all merit that comes from the study of the scriptures, from sacrifice, from austerities and charity, and reaches the Supreme Primeval Abode.

Thus, in the Holy Book the Bhagavad Gita, one of the Upanishads, in the Science of the Supreme Spirit, in the Art of Self-Knowledge, in the Colloquy between the Divine Lord Shri Krishna and the Prince Arjuna, stand the eighth chapter, entitled: The Life Everlasting.

NINE: THE SCIENCE OF SCIENCES AND THE MYSTERY OF MYSTERIES

Lord Shri Krishna said: I will now reveal to thee, since thou doubtest not, that profound mysticism, which when followed by experience, shall liberate thee from sin.

This is the Premier Science, the Sovereign Secret, the Purest and Best; intuitional, righteous; and to him who practiseth it pleasant beyond measure.

They who have no faith in this teaching cannot find Me, but remain lost in the purlieus of this perishable world.

The whole world is pervaded by Me, yet My form is not seen. All living things have their being in Me, yet I am not limited by them.

Nevertheless, they do not consciously abide in Me. Such is My Divine Sovereignty that though I, the Supreme Self, am the cause and upholder of all, yet I remain outside.

As the mighty wind, though moving everywhere, has no resting place but space, so have all these beings no home but Me.

All beings, O Arjuna, return at the close of every cosmic cycle into the realm of Nature, which is a part of Me, and at the beginning of the next I send them forth again.

With the help of Nature, again and again I pour forth the whole multitude of beings, whether they will or no, for they are ruled by My Will.

But these acts of mine do not bind Me. I remain outside and unattached.

Under my guidance, Nature produces all things movable and immovable. Thus it is, O Arjuna, that this universe revolves.

Fools disregard Me, seeing Me clad in human form. They know not that in My higher nature I am the Lord-God of all.

Their hopes are vain, their actions worthless, their knowledge futile; they are without sense, deceitful, barbarous and godless.

But the Great Souls, O Arjuna! Filled with My Divine Spirit, they worship Me, they fix their minds on Me and on Me alone, for they know that I am the imperishable Source of being.

Always extolling Me, strenuous, firm in their vows, prostrating themselves before Me, they worship Me continually with concentrated devotion.

Others worship Me with full consciousness as the One, the Manifold, the Omnipresent, the Universal.

I am the Oblation, the Sacrifice and the Worship; I am the Fuel and the Chant, I am the Butter offered to the fire, I am the Fire itself, and I am the Act of offering.

I am the Father of the universe and its Mother; I am its Nourisher and its Grandfather; I am the Knowable and the Pure; I am Om; and I am the Sacred Scriptures.

I am the Goal, the Sustainer, the Lord, the Witness, the Home, the Shelter, the Lover and the Origin; I am Life and Death; I am the Fountain and the Seed Imperishable.

I am the Heat of the Sun, I release and hold back the Rains. I am Death and Immortality; I am Being and Not-Being.

Those who are versed in the scriptures, who drink the mystic Soma-juice and are purified from sin, but who while worshipping Me with sacrifices pray that I will lead them to heaven; they reach the holy world where lives the Controller of the Powers of Nature, and they enjoy the feasts of Paradise.

Yet although they enjoy the spacious glories of Paradise, nevertheless, when their merit is exhausted, they are born again into this world of mortals. They have followed the letter of the scriptures, yet because they have sought but to fulfill their own desires, they must depart and return again and again.

But if a man will meditate on Me and Me alone, and will worship Me always and everywhere, I will take upon Myself the fulfillment of his aspiration, and I will safeguard whatsoever he shall attain.

Even those who worship the lesser Powers, if they do so with faith, they thereby worship Me, though not in the right way.

I am the willing recipient of sacrifice, and I am its true Lord. But these do not know me in truth, and so they sink back.

The votaries of the lesser Powers go to them; the devotees of spirits go to them; they who worship the Powers of Darkness, to such Powers shall they go; and so, too, those who worship Me shall come to Me.

Whatever a man offers to Me, whether it be a leaf, or a flower, of fruit, or water, I accept it, for it is offered with devotion and purity of mind.

Whatever thou doest, whatever thou dost eat, whatever thou dost sacrifice and give, whatever austerities thou practisest, do all as an offering to Me.

So shall thy action be attended by no result, either good or bad; but through the spirit of renunciation thou shalt come to Me and be free.

I am the same to all beings. I favour none, and I hate none. But those who worship Me devotedly, they live in Me, and I in them.

Even the most sinful, if he worships Me with his whole heart, shalt be considered righteous, for he is treading the right path.

He shall attain spirituality ere long, and Eternal Peace shall be his. O Arjuna! Believe me, My devotee is never lost.

For even the children of sinful parents, and those miscalled the weaker sex, and merchants, and labourers, if only they will make Me their refuge, they shall attain the Highest.

What need then to mention the holy Ministers of God, the devotees and the saintly rulers? Do thou, therefore, born in this changing and miserable world, do thou too worship Me.

Fix thy mind on Me, devote thyself to Me, sacrifice for Me, surrender to Me, make Me the object of thy aspirations, and thou shalt assuredly become one with Me, Who am thine own Self.

Thus, in the Holy Book the Bhagavad Gita, one of the Upanishads, in the Science of the Supreme Spirit, in the Art of Self-Knowledge, in the colloquy between the Divine Lord Shri Krishna and the Prince Arjuna, stands the ninth chapter, entitled: The Science of Sciences and the Mystery of Mysteries.

TEN: THE DIVINE MANIFESTATIONS

Lord Shri Krishna said: Now, O Prince! Listen to My supreme advice, which I give thee for the sake of thy welfare, for thou art My beloved.

Neither the professors of divinity nor the great ascetics know My origin, for I am the source of them all.

He who knows Me as the unborn, without beginning, the Lord of the universe, he, stripped of his delusion, becomes free from all conceivable sin.

Intelligence, wisdom, non-illusion, forgiveness, truth, self-control, calmness, pleasure, pain, birth, death, fear and fearlessness;

Harmlessness, equanimity, contentment, austerity, beneficence, fame and failure, all these, the characteristics of beings, spring from Me only.

The seven Great Seers [Mareechi, Atri, Angira, Pulah, Kratu, Pulastya, Vahishta], the Progenitors of mankind, the Ancient Four [The Masters: Sanak, Sanandan, Sanatan, Sanatkumar], and the Lawgivers were born of My Will and come forth direct from Me. The race of mankind has sprung from them.

He who rightly understands My manifested glory and My Creative Power, beyond doubt attains perfect peace.

I am the source of all; from Me everything flows. Therefore the wise worship Me with unchanging devotion.

With minds concentrated on Me, with lives absorbed in Me, and enlightening each other, they ever feel content and happy.

To those who are always devout and who worship Me with love,

I give the power of discrimination, which leads them to Me.

By My grace, I live in their hearts; and I dispel the darkness of ignorance by the shining light of wisdom.

Arjuna asked: Thou art the Supreme Spirit, the Eternal Home, the Holiest of the Holy, the Eternal Divine Self, the Primal God, the Unborn and the Omnipresent.

So have said the seers and the divine sage Narada; as well as Asita, Devala and Vyasa; and Thou Thyself also sayest it.

I believe in what Thou hast said, my Lord! For neither the godly not the godless comprehend Thy manifestation.

Thou alone knowest Thyself, by the power of Thy Self; Thou the Supreme Spirit, the Source and Master of all being, the Lord of Lords, the Ruler of the Universe.

Please tell me all about Thy glorious manifestations, by means of which Thou pervadest the world.

O Master! How shall I, by constant meditation, know Thee? My Lord! What are Thy various manifestations through which I am to mediate on Thee?

Tell me again, I pray, about the fullness of Thy power and Thy glory; for I feel that I am never satisfied when I listen to Thy immortal words.

Lord Shri Krishna replied: So be it, My beloved fried! I will unfold to thee some of the chief aspects of My glory. Of its full extent there is no end.

O Arjuna! I am the Self, seated in the hearts of all beings; I am the beginning and the life, and I am the end of them all.

Of all the creative Powers I am the Creator, of luminaries the Sun;

the Whirlwind among the winds, and the Moon among planets.

Of the Vedas I am the Hymns, I am the Electric Force in the Powers of Nature; of the senses I am the Mind; and I am the Intelligence in all that lives.

Among Forces of Vitality I am the life, I am Mammon to the heathen and the godless; I am the Energy in fire, earth, wind, sky, heaven, sun, moon and planets; and among mountains I am the Mount Meru.

Among the priests, know, O Arjuna, that I am the Apostle Brihaspati; of generals I am Skanda, the Commander-in-Chief, and of waters I am the Ocean.

Of the great seers I am Bhrigu, of words I am Om, of offerings I am the silent prayer, among things immovable I am the Himalayas.

Of trees I am the sacred Fig-tree, of the Divine Seers Narada, of the heavenly singers I am Chitraratha, their Leader, and of sages I am Kapila.

Know that among horses I am Pegasus, the heaven-born; among the lordly elephants I am the White one, and I am the Ruler among men.

I am the Thunderbolt among weapons; of cows I am the Cow of Plenty, I am Passion in those who procreate, and I am the Cobra among serpents.

I am the King-python among snakes, I am the Aqueous Principle among those that live in water, I am the Father of fathers, and among rulers I am Death.

And I am the devotee Prahlad among the heathen; of Time I am the Eternal Present; I am the Lion among beasts and the Eagle among birds.

I am the Wind among purifiers, the King Rama among warriors; I am the Crocodile among the fishes, and I am the Ganges among rivers.

I am the Beginning, the Middle and the End in creation; among sciences, I am the science of Spirituality; I am the Discussion among disputants.

Of letters I am A; I am the copulative in compound words; I am Time inexhaustible; and I am the all-pervading Preserver.

I am all-devouring Death; I am the Origin of all that shall happen; I am Fame, Fortune, Speech, Memory, Intellect, Constancy and Forgiveness.

Of hymns I am Brihatsama, of metres I am Garatri, among the months I am Margasheersha (December), and I am the Spring among seasons.

I am the Gambling of the cheat and the Splendor of the splendid; I am Victory; I am Effort; and I am the Purity of the pure.

I am Shri Krishna among the Vishnu-clan and Arjuna among the Pandavas; of the saints I am Vyasa, and I am Shukracharya among the sages.

I am the Sceptre of rulers, the Strategy of the conquerors, the Silence of mystery, the Wisdom of the wise.

I am the Seed of all being, O Arjuna! No creature moving or unmoving can live without Me.

O Arjuna! The aspects of My divine life are endless. I have mentioned but a few by way of illustration.

Whatever is glorious, excellent, beautiful and mighty, be assured that it comes from a fragment of My splendor.

But what is the use of all these details to thee? O Arjuna! I sustain this universe with only small part of Myself.

Thus, in the Holy Book the Bhagavad Gita, one of the Upanishads, in the Science of the Supreme Spirit, in the Art of Self-Knowledge, in the colloquy between the Divine Lord Shri Krishna and the Prince Arjuna, stands the tenth chapter, entitled: The Divine Manifestations.

ELEVEN: THE COSMIC VISION

Arjuna said: My Lord! Thy words concerning the Supreme Secret of Self, given for my blessing, have dispelled the illusions which surrounded me.

O Lord, whose eyes are like the lotus petal! Thou hast described in detail the origin and the dissolution of being, and Thine own Eternal Majesty.

I believe all as Thou hast declared it. I long now to have a vision of thy Divine Form, O Thou Most High!

If Thou thinkest that it can be made possible for me to see it, show me, O Lord of Lords, Thine own Eternal Self.

Lord Shri Krishna replied: Behold, O Arjuna! My celestial forms, by hundred and thousands, various in kind, in colour and in shape.

Behold thou the Powers of Nature: fire, earth, wind and sky; the sun, the heavens, the moon, the stars; all forces of vitality and of healing; and the roving winds. See the myriad wonders revealed to none but thee.

Here in Me living as one, O Arjuna, behold the whole universe, movable and immovable, and anything else that thou wouldst see!

Yet since with mortal eyes thou canst not see Me, lo! I give thee the Divine Sight. See now the glory of My Sovereignty."

Sanjaya continued: "Having thus spoken, O King, the Lord Shri Krishna, the Almighty Prince of Wisdom, showed to Arjuna the Supreme Form of the Great God.

There were countless eyes and mouths, and mystic forms innumerable, with shining ornaments and flaming celestial weapons.

Crowned with heavenly garlands, clothed in shining garments, anointed with divine unctions, He showed Himself as the Resplendent One, Marvellous, Boundless, Omnipresent.

Could a thousand suns blaze forth together it would be but a faint reflection of the radiance of the Lord God.

In that vision Arjuna saw the universe, with its manifold shapes, all embraced in One, its Supreme Lord.

Thereupon Arjuna, dumb with awe, his hair on end, his head bowed, his hands clasped in salutation, addressed the Lord thus:

Arjuna said: O almighty God! I see in Thee the powers of Nature, the various creatures of the world, the Progenitor on his lotus throne, the Sages and the shining angels.

I see Thee, infinite in form, with, as it were, faces, eyes and limbs everywhere; no beginning, no middle, no end; O Thou Lord of the Universe, Whose Form is universal!

I see thee with the crown, the sceptre and the discus; a blaze of splendor. Scarce can I gaze on thee, so radiant thou art, glowing like the blazing fire, brilliant as the sun, immeasurable.

Imperishable art Thou, the Sole One worthy to be known, the priceless Treasure-house of the universe, the immortal Guardian of the Life Eternal, the Spirit Everlasting.

Without beginning, without middle and without end, infinite in power, Thine arms all- embracing, the sun and moon Thine eyes, Thy face beaming with the fire of sacrifice, flooding the whole universe with light.

Alone thou fillest all the quarters of the sky, earth and heaven, and the regions between. O Almighty Lord! Seeing Thy marvelous and awe-inspiring Form, the spheres tremble with fear.

The troops of celestial beings enter into Thee, some invoking Thee in fear, with folded palms; the Great Seers and Adepts sing hymns to Thy Glory, saying `All Hail.'

The Vital Forces, the Major stars, Fire, Earth, Air, Sky, Sun, Heaven, Moon and Planets; the Angels, the Guardians of the Universe, the divine Healers, the Winds, the Fathers, the Heavenly Singers; and hosts of Mammon-worshippers, demons as well as saints, are amazed.

Seeing Thy stupendous Form, O Most Mighty, with its myriad faces, its innumerable eyes and limbs and terrible jaws, I myself and all the worlds are overwhelmed with awe.

When I see Thee, touching the Heavens, glowing with color, with open mouth and wide open fiery eyes, I am terrified. O My Lord! My courage and peace of mind desert me.

When I see Thy mouths with their fearful jaws like glowing fires at the dissolution of creation, I lose all sense of place; I find no rest. Be merciful, O Lord in whom this universe abides!

All these sons of Dhritarashtra, with the hosts of princes, Bheeshma, Drona and Karna, as well as the other warrior chiefs belonging to our side;

I see them all rushing headlong into Thy mouths, with terrible tusks, horrible to behold. Some are mangled between thy jaws, with their heads crushed to atoms.

As rivers in flood surge furiously to the ocean, so these heroes, the greatest among men, fling themselves into Thy flaming mouths.

As moths fly impetuously to the flame only to be killed, so these men rush into Thy mouths to court their own destruction.

Thou seemest to swallow up the worlds, to lap them in flame. Thy glory fills the universe. Thy fierce rays beat down upon it irresistibly.

Tell me then who Thou art, that wearest this dreadful Form? I bow before Thee, O Mighty One! Have mercy, I pray, and let me see Thee as Thou wert at first. I do not know what Thou intendest.

Lord Shri Krishna replied: I have shown myself to thee as the Destroyer who lays waste the world and whose purpose is destruction. In spite of thy efforts, all these warriors gathered for battle shall not escape death.

Then gird up thy loins and conquer. Subdue thy foes and enjoy the kingdom in prosperity. I have already doomed them. Be thou my instrument, Arjuna!

Drona and Bheeshma, Jayadratha and Karna, and other brave warriors – I have condemned them all. Destroy them; fight and fear not. Thy foes shall be crushed."

Sanjaya continued: Having heard these words from the Lord Shri Krishna, the Prince Arjuna, with folded hands trembling, prostrated himself and with choking voice, bowing down again and again, and overwhelmed with awe, once more addressed the Lord.

Arjuna said: My Lord! It is natural that the world revels and rejoices when it sings the praises of Thy glory; the demons fly in fear and the saints offer Thee their salutations.

How should they do otherwise? O Thou Supremest Self, greater than the Powers of creation, the First Cause, Infinite, the Lord of Lords, the Home of the universe, Imperishable, Being and Not-Being, yet transcending both.

Thou art the Primal God, the Ancient, the Supreme Abode of this universe, the Knower, the Knowledge and the Final Home. Thou fillest everything. Thy form is infinite.

Thou art the Wind, Thou art Death, Thou art the Fire, the Water, the Moon, the Father and the Grandfather. Honour and glory to Thee a thousand and a thousand times! Again and again, salutation be to Thee, O my Lord!

Salutations to Thee in front and on every side, Thou who encompasseth me round about. Thy power is infinite; Thy majesty immeasurable; thou upholdest all things; yea, Thou Thyself art All.

Whatever I have said unto Thee in rashness, taking Thee only for a friend and addressing Thee as 'O Krishna! O Yadava! O Friend!' in thoughtless familiarity, no understanding Thy greatness;

Whatever insult I have offered to Thee in jest, in sport or in repose, in conversation or at the banquet, alone or in a multitude, I ask Thy forgiveness for them all, O Thou Who art without an equal!

For Thou art the Father of all things movable and immovable, the

Worshipful, the Master of Masters! In all the worlds there is none equal to Thee, how then superior, O Thou who standeth alone, Supreme.

Therefore I prostrate myself before Thee, O Lord! Most Adorable! I salute Thee, I ask Thy blessing. Only Thou canst be trusted to bear with me, as father to son, as friend to friend, as lover to his beloved.

I rejoice that I have seen what never man saw before; yet, O Lord! I am overwhelmed with fear. Please take again the Form I know. Be merciful, O Lord! thou Who are the Home of the whole universe.

I long to see Thee as thou wert before, with the crown, the sceptre and the discus in Thy hands; in Thy other Form, with Thy four hands, O Thou Whose arms are countless and Whose forms are infinite.

Lord Shri Krishna replied: My beloved friend! It is only through My grace and power that thou hast been able to see this vision of splendor, the Universal, the Infinite, the Original. Never has it been seen by any but thee.

Not by study of the scriptures, not by sacrifice or gift, not by ritual or rigorous austerity, is it possible for man on earth to see what thou hast seen, O thou foremost hero of the Kuru- clan!

Be not afraid or bewildered by the terrible vision. Put away thy fear and, with joyful mind, see Me once again in My usual Form.

Sanjaya continued: Having thus spoken to Arjuna, Lord Shri Krishna showed Himself again in His accustomed form; and the Mighty Lord, in gentle tones, softly consoled him who lately trembled with fear.

Arjuna said: Seeing Thee in Thy gentle human form, my Lord, I am myself again, calm once more.

Lord Shri Krishna replied: It is hard to see this vision of Me that thou hast seen. Even the most powerful have longed for it in vain.

Not by study of the scriptures, or by austerities, not by gifts or sacrifices, is it possible to see Me as thou hast done.

Only by tireless devotion can I be seen and known; only thus can a man become one with Me, O Arjuna!

He whose every action is done for My sake, to whom I am the final goal, who loves Me only and hates no one – O My dearest son, only he can realize Me!

Thus, in the Holy Book the Bhagavad Gita, one of the Upanishads, in the Science of the Supreme Spirit, in the Art of Self-Knowledge, in the colloquy between the Divine Lord Shri Krishna and the Prince Arjuna, stands the eleventh chapter, entitled: The Cosmic Vision.

TWELVE: BHAKTI-YOGA – THE PATH OF LOVE

Arjuna asked: My Lord! Which are the better devotees who worship Thee, those who try to know Thee as a Personal God, or those who worship Thee as Impersonal and Indestructible?

Lord Shri Krishna replied: Those who keep their minds fixed on Me, who worship Me always with unwavering faith and concentration; these are the very best.

Those who worship Me as the Indestructible, the Undefinable, the Omnipresent, the Unthinkable, the Primeval, the Immutable and the Eternal;

Subduing their senses, viewing all conditions of life with the same eye, and working for the welfare of all beings, assuredly they come to Me.

But they who thus fix their attention on the Absolute and Impersonal encounter greater hardships, for it is difficult for those who possess a body to realize Me as without one.

Verily, those who surrender their actions to Me, who muse on Me, worship Me and meditate on Me alone, with no thought save of Me,

O Arjuna! I rescue them from the ocean of life and death, for their minds are fixed on Me. Then let thy mind cling only to Me, let thy intellect abide in Me; and without doubt thou shalt live hereafter in Me alone.

But if thou canst not fix thy mind firmly on Me, then, My beloved friend, try to do so by constant practice.

And if thou are not strong enough to practise concentration, then devote thyself to My service, do all thine acts for My sake, and thou shalt still attain the goal.

And if thou art too weak even for this, then seek refuge in union with Me, and with perfect self-control renounce the fruit of thy action.

Knowledge is superior to blind action, meditation to mere knowledge, renunciation of the fruit of action to meditation, and where there is renunciation peace will follow.

He who is incapable of hatred towards any being, who is kind and compassionate, free from selfishness, without pride, equable in pleasure and in pain, and forgiving,

Always contented, self-centred, self-controlled, resolute, with mind and reason dedicated to Me, such a devotee of Mine is My beloved.

He who does not harm the world, and whom the world cannot harm, who is not carried away by any impulse of joy, anger or fear, such a one is My beloved.

He who expects nothing, who is pure, watchful, indifferent, unruffled, and who renounces all initiative, such a one is My beloved.

He who is beyond joy and hate, who neither laments nor desires, to whom good and evil fortunes are the same, such a one is My beloved.

He to whom friend and foe are alike, who welcomes equally honor and dishonor, heat and cold, pleasure and pain, who is enamored of nothing,

Who is indifferent to praise and censure, who enjoys silence, who is contented with every fate, who has no fixed abode, who is steadfast in mind, and filled with devotion, such a one is My beloved.

Verily those who love the spiritual wisdom as I have taught, whose faith never fails, and who concentrate their whole nature on Me, they indeed are My most beloved.

Thus, in the Holy Book the Bhagavad Gita, one of the Upanishads, in the Science of the Supreme Spirit, in the Art of Self-Knowledge, in the colloquy between the Divine Lord Shri Krishna and the Prince Arjuna, stands the twelfth chapter, entitled: Bhakti-Yoga or the Path of Love.

THIRTEEN: SPIRIT AND MATTER

Arjuna asked: My Lord! Who is God and what is Nature; what is Matter and what is the Self; what is that they call Wisdom, and what is it that is worth knowing? I wish to have this explained.

Lord Shri Krishna replied: O Arjuna! The body of man is the playground of the Self; and That which knows the activities of Matter, sages call the Self.

I am the Omniscient self that abides in the playground of Matter; knowledge of Matter and of the all-knowing Self is wisdom.

What is called Matter, of what it is composed, whence it came, and why it changes, what the Self is, and what Its power – this I will now briefly set forth.

Seers have sung of It in various ways, in many hymns and sacred Vedic songs, weighty in thought and convincing in argument.

The five great fundamentals (earth, fire, air, water and ether), personality, intellect, the mysterious life force, the ten organs of perception and action, the mind and the five domains of sensation;

Desire, aversion, pleasure, pain, sympathy, vitality and the persistent clinging to life, these are in brief the constituents of changing Matter.

Humility, sincerity, harmlessness, forgiveness, rectitude, service of the Master, purity, steadfastness, self-control;

Renunciation of the delights of sense, absence of pride, right understanding of the painful problem of birth and death, of age and sickness;

Indifference, non-attachment to sex, progeny or home, equanimity in good fortune and in bad;

Unswerving devotion to Me, by concentration on Me and Me alone, a love for solitude, indifference to social life;

Constant yearning for the knowledge of Self, and pondering over the lessons of the great

Truth – this is Wisdom, all else ignorance.

I will speak to thee now of that great Truth which man ought to know, since by its means he will win immortal bliss – that which is without beginning, the Eternal Spirit which dwells in Me, neither with form, nor yet without it.

Everywhere are Its hands and Its feet; everywhere It has eyes that see, heads that think and mouths that speak; everywhere It listens; It dwells in all the worlds; It envelops them all.

Beyond the senses, It yet shines through every sense perception. Bound to nothing, It yet sustains everything. Unaffected by the Qualities, It still enjoys them all.

It is within all beings, yet outside; motionless yet moving; too subtle to be perceived; far away yet always near.

In all beings undivided, yet living in division, It is the upholder of all, Creator and Destroyer alike;

It is the Light of lights, beyond the reach of darkness; the Wisdom, the only thing that is worth knowing or that wisdom can teach; the Presence in the hearts of all.

Thus I have told thee in brief what Matter is, and the Self worth realizing and what is Wisdom. He who is devoted to Me knows; and assuredly he will enter into Me.

Know thou further that Nature and God have no beginning; and that differences of character and quality have their origin in Nature only.

Nature is the Law which generates cause and effect; God is the source of the enjoyment of all pleasure and pain.

God dwelling in the heart of Nature experiences the Qualities which nature brings forth; and His affinity towards the Qualities is the reason for His living in a good or evil body.

Thus in the body of man dwells the Supreme God; He who sees and permits, upholds and enjoys, the Highest God and the Highest Self.

He who understands God and Nature along with her qualities, whatever be his condition in life, he comes not again to earth.

Some realize the Supreme by meditating, by its aid, on the Self within, others by pure reason, others by right action.

Others again, having no direct knowledge but only hearing from others, nevertheless worship, and they, too, if true to the teachings, cross the sea of death.

Wherever life is seen in things movable or immovable, it is the joint product of Matter and Spirit.

He who can see the Supreme Lord in all beings, the Imperishable amidst the perishable, he it is who really sees.

Beholding the Lord in all things equally, his actions do not mar his spiritual life but lead him to the height of Bliss.

He who understands that it is only the Law of Nature that brings action to fruition, and that the Self never acts, alone knows the Truth.

He who sees the diverse forms of life all rooted in One, and growing forth from Him, he shall indeed find the Absolute.

The Supreme Spirit, O Prince, is without beginning, without

Qualities and Imperishable, and though it be within the body, yet It does not act, nor is It affected by action.

As space, though present everywhere, remains by reason of its subtlety unaffected, so the

Self, though present in all forms, retains its purity unalloyed.

As the one Sun illuminates the whole earth, so the Lord illumines the whole universe.

Those who with the eyes of wisdom thus see the difference between Matter and Spirit, and know how to liberate Life from the Law of Nature, they attain the Supreme.

Thus, in the Holy Book the Bhagavad Gita, one of the Upanishads, in the Science of the Supreme Spirit, in the Art of Self-Knowledge, in the colloquy between the Divine Lord Shri Krishna and the Prince Arjuna, stands the thirteenth chapter, entitled: Spirit and Matter.

FOURTEEN: THE THREE QUALITIES

Lord Shri Krishna continued: Now I will reveal unto the Wisdom which is beyond knowledge, by attaining which the sages have reached Perfection.

Dwelling in Wisdom and realizing My Divinity, they are not born again when the universe is re-created at the beginning of every cycle, nor are they affected when it is dissolved.

The eternal Cosmos is My womb, in which I plant the seed, from which all beings are born, O Prince!

O illustrious son of Kunti! Through whatever wombs men are born, it is the Spirit Itself that conceives, and I am their Father.

Purity, Passion and Ignorance are the Qualities which the Law of nature bringeth forth. They fetter the free Spirit in all beings.

O Sinless One! Of these, Purity, being luminous, strong and invulnerable, binds one by its yearning for happiness and illumination.

Passion, engendered by thirst for pleasure and attachment, binds the soul through its fondness for activity.

But Ignorance, the product of darkness, stupefies the senses in all embodied beings, binding them by chains of folly, indolence and lethargy.

Purity brings happiness, Passion commotion, and Ignorance, which obscures wisdom, leads to a life of failure.

O Prince! Purity prevails when Passion and Ignorance are overcome; Passion, when Purity and Ignorance are overcome; and Ignorance when it overcomes Purity and Passion.

When the light of knowledge gleams forth from all the gates of the body, then be sure that Purity prevails.

O best of Indians! Avarice, the impulse to act and the beginning of action itself are all due to the dominance of Passion.

Darkness, stagnation, folly and infatuation are the result of the dominance of Ignorance, O joy of the Kuru-clan!

When Purity prevails, the soul on quitting the body passes on to the pure regions where live those who know the Highest.

When Passion prevails, the soul is reborn among those who love activity; when Ignorance rules, it enters the wombs of the ignorant.

They say the fruit of a meritorious action is spotless and full of purity; the outcome of Passion is misery, and of Ignorance darkness.

Purity engenders Wisdom, Passion avarice, and Ignorance folly, infatuation and darkness.

When Purity is in the ascendant, the man evolves; when Passion, he neither evolves nor degenerates; when Ignorance, he is lost.

As soon as man understands that it is only the Qualities which act and nothing else, and perceives That which is beyond, he attains My divine nature.

When the soul transcends the Qualities, which are the real cause of physical existence, then, freed from birth and death, from old age and misery, he quaffs the nectar of immortality.

Arjuna asked: My Lord! By what signs can he who has transcended the Qualities be recognized? How does he act? How does he live beyond them?

Lord Shri Krishna replied: O Prince! He who shuns not the Quality which is present, and longs not for that which is absent;

He who maintains an attitude of indifference, who is not disturbed by the Qualities, who realizes that it is only they who act, and remains calm;

Who accepts pain and pleasure as it comes, is centered in his Self, to whom a piece of clay or stone or gold are the same, who neither likes nor dislikes, who is steadfast, indifferent alike to praise or censure;

Who looks equally upon honor and dishonor, loves friends and foes alike, abandons all initiative, such is he who transcends the Qualities.

And he who serves Me and only Me, with unfaltering devotion, shall overcome the Qualities, and become One with the Eternal.

For I am the Home of the Spirit, the continual Source of immortality, of eternal Righteousness and of infinite Joy.

Thus, in the Holy Book the Bhagavad Gita, one of the Upanishads, in the Science of the Supreme Spirit, in the Art of Self-Knowledge, in the colloquy between the Divine Lord Shri Krishna and the Prince Arjuna, stands the fourteenth chapter, entitled: The Three Qualities.

FIFTEEN: THE LORD-GOD

Lord Shri Krishna continued: This phenomenal creation, which is both ephemeral and eternal, is like a tree, but having its seed above in the Highest and its ramifications on this earth below. The scriptures are its leaves, and he who understands this, knows.

Its branches shoot upwards and downwards, deriving their nourishment from the Qualities; its buds are the objects of sense; and its roots, which follow the Law causing man's regeneration and degeneration, pierce downwards into the soil.

In this world its true form is not known, neither its origin nor its end, and its strength is not understood., until the tree with its roots striking deep into the earth is hewn down by the sharp axe of non-attachment.

Beyond lies the Path, from which, when found, there is no return. This is the Primal God from whence this ancient creation has sprung.

The wise attain Eternity when, freed from pride and delusion, they have conquered their love for the things of sense; when, renouncing desire and fixing their gaze on the Self, they have ceased to be tossed to and fro by the opposing sensations, like pleasure and pain.

Neither sun, moon, nor fire shines there. Those who go thither never come back. For, O Arjuna, that is my Celestial Home!

It is only a very small part of My Eternal Self, which is the life of the universe, drawing round itself the six senses, the mind the last, which have their source in Nature.

When the Supreme Lord enters a body or leaves it, He gathers these senses together and travels on with them, as the wind gathers perfume while passing through the flowers.

He is the perception of the ear, the eye, the touch, the taste and the smell, yea and of the mind also; and the enjoyment the things which they perceive is also His.

The ignorant do not see that it is He Who is present in life and Who departs at death or even that it is He Who enjoys pleasure through the Qualities. Only the eye of wisdom sees.

The saints with great effort find Him within themselves; but not the unintelligent, who in spite of every effort cannot control their minds.

Remember that the Light which, proceeding from the sun, illumines the whole world, and the Light which is in the moon, and That which is in the fire also, all are born of Me.

I enter this world and animate all My creatures with My vitality; and by My cool moonbeams I nourish the plants.

Becoming the fire of life, I pass into their bodies and, uniting with the vital streams of Prana and Apana, I digest the various kinds of food.

I am enthroned in the hearts of all; memory, wisdom and discrimination owe their origins to Me. I am He Who is to be realized in the scriptures; I inspire their wisdom and I know their truth.

There are two aspects in Nature: the perishable and the imperishable. All life in this world belongs to the former, the unchanging element belongs to the latter.

But higher than all am I, the Supreme God, the Absolute Self, the Eternal Lord, Who pervades the worlds and upholds them all.

Beyond comparison of the Eternal with the non-eternal am I, Who am called by scriptures and sages the Supreme Personality, the Highest God.

He who with unclouded vision sees Me as the Lord-God, knows all there is to be known, and always shall worship Me with his whole heart.

Thus, O Sinless One, I have revealed to thee this most mystic knowledge. He who understands gains wisdom and attains the consummation of life.

Thus, in the Holy Book the Bhagavad Gita, one of the Upanishads, in the Science of the Supreme Spirit, in the Art of Self-

Knowledge, in the colloquy between the Divine Lord Shri Krishna and the Prince Arjuna, stands the fifteenth chapter, entitled: The Lord-God

SIXTEEN: DIVINE AND DEMONIC CIVILIZATION

Lord Shri Krishna continued: Fearlessness, clean living, unceasing concentration on wisdom, readiness to give, self-control, a spirit of sacrifice, regular study of the scriptures, austerities, candor, harmlessness, truth, absence of wrath, renunciation, contentment, straightforwardness, compassion towards all, uncovetousness, courtesy, modesty, constancy,

Valor, forgiveness, fortitude, purity, freedom from hate and vanity; these are his who possesses the Godly Qualities, O Arjuna!

Hypocrisy, pride, insolence, cruelty, ignorance belong to him who is born of the godless qualities.

Godly qualities lead to liberation; godless to bondage. Do not be anxious, Prince! Thou hast the Godly qualities.

All beings are of two classes: Godly and godless. The Godly I have described; I will now describe the other.

The godless do not know how to act or how to renounce. They have neither purity nor truth. They do not understand the right principles of conduct.

They say the universe is an accident with no purpose and no God. Life is created by sexual union, a product of lust and nothing else.

Thinking thus, these degraded souls, these enemies of mankind – whose intelligence is negligible and whose deeds are monstrous – come into the world only to destroy.

Giving themselves up to insatiable passions, hypocritical, self-sufficient and arrogant, cherishing false conception founded on delusion, they work only to carry out their own unholy purposes.

Poring anxiously over evil resolutions, which only end in death; seeking only the gratification of desire as the highest goal; seeing nothing beyond;

Caught in the toils of a hundred vain hopes, the slaves of passion and wrath, they accumulate hoards of unjust wealth, only to pander to their sensual desire.

This I have gained today; tomorrow I will gratify another desire; this wealth is mine now, the rest shall be mine ere long;

I have slain one enemy, I will slay the others also; I am worthy to enjoy, I am the Almighty, I am perfect, powerful and happy;

I am rich, I am well-bred; who is there to compare with me? I will sacrifice, I will give, I will pay – and I will enjoy. Thus blinded by Ignorance,

Perplexed by discordant thoughts, entangled in the snares of desire, infatuated by passion, they sink into the horrors of hell.

Self-conceited, stubborn, rich, proud and insolent, they make a display of their patronage, disregarding the rules of decency.

Puffed up by power and inordinate conceit, swayed by lust and wrath, these wicked people hate Me Who am within them, as I am within all.

Those who thus hate Me, who are cruel, the dregs of mankind, I condemn them to a continuous, miserable and godless rebirth.

So reborn, they spend life after life, enveloped in delusion. And they never reach Me, O Prince, but degenerate into still lower forms of life.

The gates of hell are three: lust, wrath and avarice. They destroy the Self. Avoid them. These are the gates which lead to darkness; if a man avoid them he will ensure his own welfare, and in the end will attain his liberation.

But he who neglects the commands of the scriptures, and follows the promptings of passion, he does not attain perfection, happiness or the final goal.

Therefore whenever there is doubt whether thou shouldst do a thing or not, let the scriptures guide thy conduct. In the light of the scriptures shouldst thou labor the whole of thy life.

Thus, in the Holy Book the Bhagavad Gita, one of the Upanishads, in the Science of the Supreme Spirit, in the Art of Self-Knowledge, in the colloquy between the Divine Lord Shri Krishna and the Prince Arjuna, stands the sixteenth chapter, entitled: Divine and Demonic Civilization

SEVENTEEN: THE THREEFOLD FAITH

Arjuna asked: My Lord! Those who do acts of sacrifice, not according to the scriptures but nevertheless with implicit faith, what is their condition? Is it one of Purity, of Passion or of Ignorance?

Lord Shri Krishna replied: Man has an inherent faith in one or another of the Qualities – Purity, Passion and Ignorance. Now listen.

The faith of every man conforms to his nature. By nature he is full of faith. He is in fact what his faith makes him.

The Pure worship the true God; the Passionate, the powers of wealth and magic; the Ignorant, the spirits of the dead and of the lower orders of nature.

Those who practice austerities not commanded by scripture, who are slaves to hypocrisy and egotism, who are carried away by the fury of desire and passion,

They are ignorant. They torment the organs of the body; and they harass Me also, Who lives within. Know that they are devoted to evil.

The food which men enjoy is also threefold, like the ways of sacrifice, austerity and almsgiving. Listen to the distinction.

The foods that prolong life and increase purity, vigor, health, cheerfulness and happiness are those that are delicious, soothing, substantial and agreeable. These are loved by the Pure.

Those in whom Passion is dominant like foods that are bitter, sour, salty, over-hot, pungent, dry and burning. These produce unhappiness, repentance and disease.

The Ignorant love food which is stale, not nourishing, putrid and corrupt, the leavings of others and unclean.

Sacrifice is Pure when it is offered by one who does not covet the fruit thereof, when it is done according to the commands of scripture, and with implicit faith that the sacrifice is a duty.

Sacrifice which is performed for the sake of its results, or for self-glorification – that, O best of Aryans, is the product of Passion.

Sacrifice that is contrary to scriptural command, that is unaccompanied by prayers or gifts of food or money, and is without faith – that is the product of Ignorance.

Worship of God and the Master; respect for the preacher and the philosopher; purity, rectitude, continence and harmlessness – all this is physical austerity.

Speech that hurts no one, that is true, is pleasant to listen to and beneficial, and the constant study of the scriptures – this is austerity in speech.

Serenity, kindness, silence, self-control and purity – this is austerity of mind.

These threefold austerities performed with faith, and without thought of reward, may truly be accounted Pure.

Austerity coupled with hypocrisy or performed for the sake of self-glorification, popularity or vanity, comes from Passion, and its result is always doubtful and temporary.

Austerity done under delusion, and accompanied with sorcery or torture to oneself or another, may be assumed to spring from Ignorance.

The gift which is given without thought of recompense, in the belief that it ought to be made, in a fit place, at an opportune time and to a deserving person – such a gift is Pure.

That which is given for the sake of the results it will produce, or with the hope of recompense, or grudgingly – that may truly be said to be the outcome of Passion.

And that which is given at an unsuitable place or time or to one who is unworthy, or with disrespect or contempt – such a gift is the result of Ignorance.

"Om Tat Sat" is the triple designation of the Eternal Spirit, by which of old the Vedic Scriptures, the ceremonials and the sacrifices were ordained.

Therefore all acts of sacrifice, gifts and austerities, prescribed by the scriptures, are always begun by those who understand the Spirit with the word Om.

Those who desire deliverance begin their acts of sacrifice, austerity or gift with the word "Tat" (meaning 'That'), without thought of reward.

"Sat" means Reality or the highest Good, and also, O Arjuna, it is used to mean an action of exceptional merit.

Conviction in sacrifice, in austerity and in giving is also called "Sat." So too an action done only for the Lord's sake.

Whatsoever is done without faith, whether it be sacrifice, austerity or gift or anything else, as called "Asat" (meaning "Unreal") for it is the negation of "Sat," O Arjuna! Such an act has no significance, here or hereafter.

Thus, in the Holy Book the Bhagavad Gita, one of the Upanishads, in the Science of the Supreme Spirit, in the Art of Self-Knowledge, in the colloquy between the Divine Lord Shri Krishna and the Prince Arjuna, stands the seventeenth chapter, entitled: The Threefold Faith

EIGHTEEN: THE SPIRIT OF RENUNCIATION

Arjuna asked: O mighty One! I desire to know how relinquishment is distinguished from renunciation.

Lord Shri Krishna replied: The sages say that renunciation means forgoing an action which springs from desire; and relinquishing means the surrender of its fruit.

Some philosophers say that all action is evil and should be abandoned. Others that acts of sacrifice, benevolence and austerity should not be given up.

O best of Indians! Listen to my judgment as regards this problem. It has a threefold aspect. Acts of sacrifice, benevolence and austerity should not be given up but should be performed, for they purify the aspiring soul.

But they should be done with detachment and without thought of recompense. This is my final judgment.

It is not right to give up actions which are obligatory; and if they are misunderstood, it is the result of sheer ignorance.

To avoid an action through fear of physical suffering, because it is likely to be painful, is to act from passion, and the benefit of renunciation will not follow.

He who performs an obligatory action, because he believes it to be a duty which ought to be done, without any personal desire to do the act or to receive any return – such renunciation is Pure.

The wise man who has attained purity, whose doubts are solved, who is filled with the spirit of self-abnegation, does not shrink from action because it brings pain, nor does he desire it because it brings pleasure.

But since those still in the body cannot entirely avoid action, in their case abandonment of the fruit of action is considered as complete renunciation.

For those who cannot renounce all desire, the fruit of action hereafter is threefold – good, evil, and partly good and partly evil. But for him who has renounced, there is none.

I will tell thee now, O Mighty Man, the five causes which, according to the final decision of philosophy, must concur before an action can be accomplished.

They are a body, a personality, physical organs, their manifold activity and destiny. Whatever action a man performs, whether by muscular effort or by speech or by thought, and whether it be right or wrong, these five are the essential causes.

But the fool who supposes, because of his immature judgment, that it is his own Self alone that acts, he perverts the truth and does not see rightly.

He who has no pride, and whose intellect is unalloyed by attachment, even though he kill these people, yet he does not kill them, and his act does not bind him.

Knowledge, the knower and the object of knowledge, these are the three incentives to action; and the act, the actor and the instrument are the threefold constituents.

The knowledge, the act and the doer differ according to the Qualities. Listen to this too: That knowledge which sees the One Indestructible in all beings, the One Indivisible in all separate lives, may be truly called Pure Knowledge.

The knowledge which thinks of the manifold existence in all beings as separate – that comes from Passion.

But that which clings blindly to one idea as if it were all, without logic, truth or insight, that has its origin in Darkness.

An obligatory action done by one who is disinterested, who neither likes nor dislikes it, and gives no thought to the consequences that follow, such an action is Pure.

But even though an action involve the most strenuous endeavor, yet if the doer is seeking to gratify his desires, and is filled with personal vanity, it may be assumed to originate in Passion.

An action undertaken through delusion, and with no regard to the spiritual issues involved, or the real capacity of the doer, or to the injury which may follow, such an act may be assumed to be the product of Ignorance.

But when a man has no sentiment and no personal vanity, when he possesses courage and confidence, cares not whether he succeeds or fails, then his action arises from Purity.

In him who is impulsive, greedy, looking for reward, violent, impure, torn between joy and sorrow, it may be assumed that in him Passion is predominant.

While he whose purpose is infirm, who is low-minded, stubborn, dishonest, malicious, indolent, despondent, procrastinating – he may be assumed to be in Darkness.

Reason and conviction are threefold, according to the Quality which is dominant. I will explain them fully and severally, O Arjuna!

That intellect which understands the creation and dissolution of life, what actions should be done and what not, which discriminates between fear and fearlessness, bondage and deliverance, that is Pure.

The intellect which does not understand what is right and what is wrong, and what should be done and what not, is under the sway of Passion.

And that which, shrouded in Ignorance, thinks wrong right, and sees everything perversely, O Arjuna, that intellect is ruled by Darkness.

The conviction and steady concentration by which the mind, the vitality and the senses are controlled – O Arjuna! They are the product of Purity.

The conviction which always holds fast to rituals, to self-interest and wealth, for the sake of what they may bring forth – that comes from Passion.

And that which clings perversely to false idealism, fear, grief, despair and vanity is the product of Ignorance.

Hear further the three kinds of pleasure. That which increases day after day delivers one from misery,

Which at first seems like poison but afterwards acts like nectar – that pleasure is Pure, for it is born of Wisdom.

That which as first is like nectar, because the senses revel in their objects, but in the end acts like poison – that pleasure arises from Passion.

While the pleasure which from first to last merely drugs the senses, which springs from indolence, lethargy and folly – that pleasure flows from Ignorance.

There is nothing anywhere on earth or in the higher worlds which is free from the three Qualities – for they are born of Nature.

O Arjuna! The duties of spiritual teachers, the soldiers, the traders and the servants have all been fixed according to the dominant Quality in their nature.

Serenity, self-restraint, austerity, purity, forgiveness, as well as uprightness, knowledge, wisdom and faith in God – these constitute the duty of a spiritual Teacher.

Valor, glory, firmness, skill, generosity, steadiness in battle and ability to rule – these constitute the duty of a soldier. They flow from his own nature.

Agriculture, protection of the cow and trade are the duty of a trader, again in accordance with his nature. The duty of a servant is to serve, and that too agrees with his nature.

Perfection is attained when each attends diligently to his duty. Listen and I will tell you how it is attained by him who always minds his own duty.

Man reaches perfection by dedicating his actions to God, Who is the source of all being, and fills everything.

It is better to do one's own duty, however defective it may be, than to follow the duty of another, however well one may perform it. He who does his duty as his own nature reveals it, never sins.

The duty that of itself falls to one's lot should not be abandoned, though it may have its defects. All acts are marred by defects, as fire is obscured by smoke.

He whose mind is entirely detached, who has conquered himself, whose desires have vanished, by his renunciation reaches that stage of perfect freedom where action completes itself and leaves no seed.

I will now state briefly how he, who has reached perfection, finds the Eternal Spirit, the state of Supreme Wisdom.

Guided always by pure reason, bravely restraining himself, renouncing the objects of sense and giving up attachment and hatred;

Enjoying solitude, abstemiousness, his body, mind and speech under perfect control, absorbed in meditation, he becomes free – always filled with the spirit of renunciation.

Having abandoned selfishness, power, arrogance, anger and desire, possessing nothing of his own and having attained peace, he is fit to join the Eternal Spirit.

And when he becomes one with the Eternal, and his soul knows the bliss that belongs to the Self, he feels no desire and no regret, he regards all beings equally and enjoys the blessing of supreme devotion to Me.

By such devotion, he sees Me, who I am and what I am; and thus realizing the Truth, he enters My Kingdom.

Relying on Me in all his action and doing them for My sake, he attains, by My Grace, Eternal and Unchangeable Life.

Surrender then thy actions unto Me, live in Me, concentrate thine intellect on Me, and think always of Me.

Fix but thy mind on Me, and by My grace thou shalt overcome the obstacles in thy path. But if, misled by pride, thou wilt not listen, then indeed thou shalt be lost.

If thou in thy vanity thinkest of avoiding this fight, thy will shall not be fulfilled, for Nature herself will compel thee.

O Arjuna! Thy duty binds thee. From thine own nature has it arisen, and that which in thy delusion thou desire not to do, that very thing thou shalt do. Thou art helpless.

God dwells in the hearts of all beings, O Arjuna! He causes them to revolve as it were on a wheel by His mystic power.

With all thy strength, fly unto Him and surrender thyself, and by His grace shalt thou attain Supreme Peace and reach the Eternal Home.

Thus have I revealed to thee the Truth, the Mystery of mysteries. Having thought it over, thou art free to act as thou wilt.

Only listen once more to My last word, the deepest secret of all; thou art My beloved, thou are My friend, and I speak for thy welfare.

Dedicate thyself to Me, worship Me, sacrifice all for Me, prostrate thyself before Me, and to Me thou shalt surely come. Truly do I pledge thee; thou art My own beloved.

Give up then thy earthly duties, surrender thyself to Me only. Do not be anxious; I will absolve thee from all thy sin.

Speak not this to one who has not practiced austerities, or to him who does not love, or who will not listen, or who mocks.

But he who teaches this great secret to My devotees, his is the highest devotion, and verily he shall come unto Me.

Nor is there among men any who can perform a service dearer to Me than this, or any man on earth more beloved by Me than he.

He who will study this spiritual discourse of ours, I assure thee, he shall thereby worship Me at the altar of Wisdom.

Yea, he who listens to it with faith and without doubt, even he, freed from evil, shalt rise to the worlds which the virtuous attain through righteous deeds.

O Arjuna! Hast thou listened attentively to My words? Has thy ignorance and thy delusion gone?

Arjuna replied: My Lord! O Immutable One! My delusion has

fled. By Thy Grace, O Changeless One, the light has dawned. My doubts are gone, and I stand before Thee ready to do Thy will.

Sanjaya told: "Thus have I heard this rare, wonderful and soul-stirring discourse of the Lord Shri Krishna and the great-souled Arjuna.

Through the blessing of the sage Vyasa, I listened to this secret and noble science from the lips of its Master, the Lord Shri Krishna.

O King! The more I think of that marvelous and holy discourse, the more I lose myself in joy.

As memory recalls again and again the exceeding beauty of the Lord, I am filled with amazement and happiness.

Wherever is the Lord Shri Krishna, the Prince of Wisdom, and wherever is Arjuna, the Great Archer, I am more than convinced that good fortune, victory, happiness and righteousness will follow"

Thus, in the Holy Book the Bhagavad Gita, one of the Upanishads, in the Science of the Supreme Spirit, in the Art of Self-Knowledge, in the colloquy between the Divine Lord Shri Krishna and the Prince Arjuna, stands the eighteenth chapter, entitled: The Spirit of Renunciation

May the Lord Shri Krishna bless you!

The Ten Principal Upanishads

Translated by

Shri Purohit Swami

Preface

Incompetent to expound Indian philosophy, I shall illustrate some few things that have to be said from my own daily thoughts and contemporary poetry.

Shree Purohit Swami has asked me to introduce what is twice as much his as mine, for he knows Sanskrit and English, I but English. Before, after and during his nine years' pilgrimage round India he has sung in Sanskrit every morning the Awadhoota Geeta, attributed to Dattatreya, an ancient Sage to whom he pays particular devotion, and two Upanishads, the Sad-guru, his own composition, and the Mandookya; and perhaps at night to entertain or edify his hosts, songs of his own composition - those in Marathi or Hindi among the unlearned, those in Sanskrit among the learned. Sanskrit has been a familiar speech, not changing from place to place, but always on his tongue.

For some forty years my friend George Russell (A.E.) has quoted me passages from some Upanishad, and for those forty years I have said to myself—some day I will find out if he knows what he is talking about. Between us existed from the beginning the antagonism that unites dear friends. More than once I asked him the name of some translator and even bought the book, but the most eminent scholars left me incredulous. Could latinised words, hyphenated words ; could polyglot phrases, sedentary distortions of unnatural English:— 'However many Gods in Thee, All-Knower, adversely slay desires of a person'—could muddles, muddied by 'Lo! Verily' and 'Forsooth', represent what grass farmers sang thousands of years ago, what their descendants sing today? So when I met Shree Purohit Swami I proposed that we should go to India and make a translation that would read as though the original had been written in common English: 'To write well,' said Aristotle, 'express yourself like the common people, but think like a wise man', a favourite quotation of Lady Gregory's—I quote her diary from memory. Then when lack of health and money made India impossible we chose Majorca to escape telephones and foul weather, and there the work was done, not, as I had planned, in ease and leisure, but in the interstices left me by a long illness. Yet I am satisfied; I have escaped that polyglot, hyphenated, latinised, muddied muddle of distortion that froze belief. Can we believe or disbelieve until we have put our thought into a language wherein we are accustomed to express love and hate and all the shades between? When belief comes we stand up, walk up and down, laugh or swing an arm; a mathematician gets drunk ; finding that which is the prerogative of men of action.

I have not worked to confound George Russell, though often saddened by the thought that I could not —he died some months ago—but to confound something in myself. He expressed in his ceaseless vague preoccupation with the East a need and curiosity of our time,' Psychical research, which must some day deeply concern religious philosophy, for its evidences surround the pilgrim and the devotee though they never take the centre of the stage, has already proved the existence of faculties that would, combined into one man, make of that man a miracle-working Yogi. More and more too does it seem to approach a main thought of the Upanishads. Continental investigators, who reject the spiritism of Lodge and Crookes, but accept their phenomena, postulate an individual self-possessed of such power and knowledge that they seem at every moment about to identify it with that Self without limitation and sorrow, containing and contained by all, and to seek there not only the living but the dead.

But our need and curiosity have no one source. Between 1922 and 1925 English literature, wherever most intense, cast off its preoccupation with social problems and began to create myths like those of antiquity, and to ask the most profound questions. I recall poems by T. S. Eliot, Those Barren Leaves' by Aldous Huxley, where there is a Buddhistic hatred of life, or a hatred

Schopenhauer did not so much find in as deduced from a Latin translation of a Persian translation of the Upanishads: certain poems—The Seven Days of the Sun', 'Matrix', The Mutations of the Phoenix', by W. J. Turner, by Dorothy Wellesley, by Herbert Read, which have displayed in myths, not as might some writer of my youth for the sake of romantic suggestion but urged by the most recent thought, the world emerging from the human mind. A still younger generation has brought a more minute psychological curiosity, suggesting an eye where a goldsmith's magnifying glass is screwed, to like preoccupations.

In their pursuit of meaning, Day Lewis, MacNeice, Auden, Laura Riding have thrown off too much, as I think, the old metaphors, the sensuous tradition of the poets:

High on some mountain shelf

Huddle the pitiless abstractions bald about the neck

but have found, perhaps the more easily for that sacrifice, a neighborhood where some new Upanishad, some half-asiatic masterpiece, may start up amid our averted eyes.

When I was young we talked much of tradition, and those emotional young men, Francis Thompson, Lionel Johnson, John Gray, found it in Christianity. But now that *The Golden Bough* has made Christianity look modern and fragmentary we study Confucius with Ezra Pound, or like T. S. Eliot find in Christianity a convenient symbolism for some older or newer thought, or say with Henry Airbubble, 'I am a member of the Church of England but not a Christian.' Shree Purohit Swami and I offer to some young man seeking, like Shakespeare, Dante, Milton, vast sentiments and generalisations, the oldest philosophical compositions of the world, compositions, not writings, for they were sung long before they were written down. European scholarship with many doubts has fixed their date, or the date of the most important, as a little before 600 B.c. when Buddha was born, but Indian scholarship prefers a far earlier date. Whatever the date, those forest Sages began everything; no fundamental problem of philosophy, nothing that has disturbed the schools to controversy, escaped their notice.

It pleases me to fancy that when we turn towards the East, in or out of church, we are turning not less to the ancient west and north; the one fragment of pagan Irish philosophy come down, 'the Song of Amergin', seems Asiatic; that a system of thought like that of these books, though perhaps less perfectly organised, once overspread the world, as ours today [*All Indian clerks in Government offices have just been ordered to wear trousers, so at any rate declares a London merchant, an exporter to India, who has decided to specialise in trouser-stretchers. It follows the flag.*] that our genuflections discover in that East something ancestral in ourselves, something we must bring into the light before we can appease a religious instinct that for the first time in our civilisation demands the satisfaction of the whole man.

Upanishad is doctrine or wisdom (literally 'At the feet of', meaning thereby 'At the feet of some Master'), the doctrine or wisdom of the Wedas. Each is attached to some section and sometimes is named from the section. The Katha-Upanishad for instance is part of the Kathak Brahman section in the Yajur-Weda. Shree Purohit Swami has omitted the usual first five chapters of the Chhand6gya-Upanishad because they are so intermixed with ritual that they are no longer studied, though still sung. For the same reason he has selected from Briha-daranyaka-Upanishad such passages as contain no such intermixture. A few passages have been 'omitted, not because descriptions of ritual but because repetitions of what is said and said as well elsewhere. Their order wherein the Upanishads should be studied, according to tradition, is that in which they are printed in this book.

W. B. YEATS.

Contents

1. The Lord [Eesha-Upanishad]

2. At Whose Command? [Kena-Upanishad]

3. From the Kathak Branch of the Wedas [Katha-Upanishad]

4. Questions [Prashna-Upanishad]

5. At the Feet of the Monk [Mundaka-Upanishad]

6. At the Feet of Master Mandooka [Mandookya-Upanishad]

7. From the Taittireeya Branch of the Wedas [Taittireeya-Upanishad]

8. At the Feet of Master Aitareya [Aitareya-Upanishad]

9. The Doctrine of the Chhandogyas [Chhandogya-Upanishad]

10. Famous Debates in the Forest [Brihadaranyaka-Upanishad

I

The Lord

Eesha Upanishad

That is perfect.

This is perfect.

Perfect comes from perfect.

Take perfect from perfect, the remainder is perfect.

May peace and peace and peace be everywhere.

Whatever lives is full of the Lord. Claim nothing; enjoy, do not covet His property.

Then hope for a hundred years of life doing your duty. No other way can prevent deeds from clinging, proud as you are of your human life.

They that deny the Self, return after death to a godless birth, blind, enveloped in darkness.

The Self is one. Unmoving, it moves faster than the mind. The senses lag, but Self runs ahead. Unmoving, it outruns pursuit. Out of Self comes the breath that is the life of all things.

Unmoving, it moves; is far away, yet near; within all, outside all.

Of a certainty the man who can see all creatures in himself, himself in all creatures, knows no sorrow.

How can a wise man, knowing the unity of life, seeing all creatures in himself, be deluded or sorrowful?

The Self is everywhere, without a body, without a shape, whole, pure, wise, all knowing, far shining, self-depending, all transcending} in the eternal procession assigning to every period its proper duty.

Pin your faith to natural knowledge, stumble through the darkness of the blind; pin your faith to supernatural knowledge, stumble through a darkness deeper still.

Natural knowledge brings one result, supernatural knowledge another. We have heard it from the wise who have clearly explained it.

They that know and can distinguish between natural knowledge and supernatural knowledge shall, by the first, cross the perishable in safety; shall, passing beyond the second, attain immortal life.

Pin your faith to the seed of nature, stumble through the darkness of the blind; pin your faith to the shapes of nature, stumble through a darkness deeper still.

The seed of nature brings one result; the shapes of nature another. We have heard it from the wise, who have clearly explained it.

They that know and can distinguish between the shapes of nature and the seed of nature shall, by the first, cross the perishable in safety; shall, passing beyond the second, attain immortal life.

They have put a golden stopper into the neck of the bottle. Pull it, Lord! Let out reality. I am full of longing.

Protector, Seer, controller of all, fountain of life, upholder, do not waste light; gather light; let me see that blessed body—'-Lord of all. I myself am He.

Life merge into the all prevalent, the eternal; body turn to ashes. Mind! meditate on the eternal Spirit; remember past deeds.

Mind! remember past deeds; remember, Mind! remember.

Holy light! illuminate the way that we may gather the good we planted. Are not our deeds known to you? Do not let us grow crooked, we that kneel and pray again and again.

II

At Whose Command?
Kena Upanishad

1

Speech, eyes, ears, limbs, life, energy, come to my help. These books have Spirit for theme. I shall never deny Spirit, nor Spirit deny me. Let me be in union, communion with Spirit. When I am one with Spirit, may the laws these books proclaim live in me, may the laws live.

The enquirer asked: What has called my mind to the hunt? What has made my life begin? What wags in my tongue? What God has opened eye and ear?

The teacher answered: It lives in all that lives, hearing through the ear, thinking through the mind, speaking through the tongue, seeing through the eye. The wise man clings neither to this nor that, rises out of sense, attains immortal life.

Eye, tongue, cannot approach it nor mind know it; not knowing, we cannot satisfy enquiry. It lies beyond the known, beyond the unknown. We know through those who have preached it, have learnt it from tradition.

That which makes the tongue speak, but needs no tongue to explain, that alone is Spirit; not what sets the world by the ears.

That which makes the mind think, but needs no mind to think, that alone is Spirit; not what sets the world by the ears.

That which makes the eye see, but needs no eye to see, that alone is Spirit; not what sets the world by the ears.

That which makes the ear hear, but needs no ear to hear, that alone is Spirit; not what sets the world by the ears.

That which makes life live, but; needs no life to live, that alone is Spirit; not what sets the world by the ears.

2

If you think that you know much, you know little. If you think that you know It from study of your own mind or of nature, study again.

The enquirer said: I do not think that I know much, I neither say that I know, nor say that I do not.

The teacher answered: The man who claims that he knows, knows nothing; but he who claims nothing, knows.

Who says that Spirit is not known, knows; who claims that he knows, knows nothing. The ignorant think that Spirit lies within knowledge, the wise man knows It beyond knowledge.

Spirit is known through revelation. It leads to freedom. It leads to power. Revelation is the conquest of death.

The living man who finds Spirit, finds Truth. But if he fails, he sinks among fouler shapes. The man who can see the same Spirit in every creature, clings neither to this nor that, attains immortal life.

3

Once upon a time, Spirit planned that the gods might win a great victory. The gods grew boastful; though Spirit had planned their victory, they thought they had done it all.

Spirit saw their vanity and appeared. They could not understand; they said: Who is that mysterious Person?

They said to Fire: Fire! Find out who is that mysterious Person.

Fire ran to Spirit. Spirit asked what it was. Fire said: I am Fire; known to all.

Spirit asked: What can you do? Fire said: I can burn anything and everything in this world.

Burn it, said Spirit, putting a straw on the ground. Fire threw itself upon the straw, but could not burn it. Then Fire ran to the gods in a hurry and confessed it could not find out who was that mysterious Person.

Then the gods asked Wind to find out who was that mysterious Person.

Wind ran to Spirit and Spirit asked what it was. Wind said: I am Wind. I am the King of the Air.

Spirit asked: What can you do? and Wind said: I can blow away anything and everything in this world.

Blow it away, said Spirit, putting a straw on the ground. Wind threw itself upon the straw, but could not move it. Then Wind ran to the gods in a hurry and confessed it could not find out who was that mysterious Person.

Then the gods went to Light and asked it to find out who was that mysterious Person. Light ran towards Spirit, but Spirit disappeared upon the instant.

There appeared in the sky that pretty girl, the Goddess of Wisdom, snowy Himalaya's daughter. Light went to her and asked who was that mysterious Person.

4

The Goddess said: 'Spirit, through Spirit you attained your greatness. Praise the greatness of Spirit.' Then Light knew that the mysterious Person was none but Spirit.

That is how these gods—Fire, Wind and Light— attained supremacy ; they came nearest to Spirit and were the first to call that Person Spirit.

Light stands above Fire and Wind; because closer than they, it was the first to call that Person Spirit.

This is the moral of the tale. In the lightning, in the light of an eye, the light belongs to Spirit.

The power of the mind when it remembers and desires, when it thinks again and again, belongs to Spirit. Therefore let Mind meditate on Spirit.

Spirit is the Good in all. It should be worshipped as the Good. He that knows it as the Good is esteemed by all.

You asked me about spiritual knowledge, I have explained it.

Austerity, self-control, meditation are the foundation of this knowledge; the Wedas are its house, truth its shrine.

He who knows this shall prevail against all evil, enjoy the Kingdom of Heaven, yes, for ever enjoy the blessed Kingdom of Heaven.

III

From the Kathak Branch of the Wedas
Kathak Upanishad

Book 1

1

May He protect us both. May He take pleasure in us both. May we show courage together. May spiritual knowledge shine before us. May we never hate one another. May peace and peace and peace be everywhere.

Wajashrawas, wanting heaven, gave away all his property.

He had a son by name Nachiketas. While the gifts were passing, Nachiketas, though but a boy, thought to himself:

He has not earned much of a heaven; his cows can neither eat, drink, calve nor give milk.

He went to his father and said: Father, have you given me to somebody? He repeated the question a second and a third time; at last his father said: I give you to Death.

Nachiketas thought: Whether I die now or later matters little; but what I would like to know is what happens if Death gets me now.

Wajashrawas would have taken back his words but Nachiketas said: Think of those who went before, those that will come after: their word their bond. Man dies and is born again like a blade of grass.

Nachiketas went into the forest and sat in meditation within the house of Death. When Death appeared his servant said: Lord! When a holy man enters a house as guest it is as if Fire entered. The wise man cools him down. So please give him water.

If a holy man comes into a fool's house and is given nothing, the fool's family, public and private life, ambitions, reputation, property, hopes, alliances, all suffer.

Thereupon Death said to Nachiketas: A guest should be respected; you have lived three days in my house without eating and drinking. I bow to you, holy man! Take from me three gifts and I shall be the better for it.

Nachiketas said: I will take as my first gift that I may be reconciled to my father; that he may be happy; that he may keep no grudge against me but make me welcome.

Death said: I shall so arrange things, that when your father gets you back he shall sleep well at night, his grudge forgotten and love you as before.

Nachiketas said: There is no fear in the Kingdom of Heaven; because you are not there, nobody there is afraid of old age; man is beyond hunger, thirst and sorrow.

Death! you know what Fire leads to heaven, show it, I am full of faith. I ask that Fire as my second gift.

Death said: I will explain it, listen. Find the rock and conquer unmeasured worlds. Listen, for this came out of the cavern.

Death told him that out of Fire comes this world, what bricks and how many go to the altar, how best to build it. Nachiketas repeated all. Death encouraged ran on:

I give you another gift. This Fire shall be called by your name.

Count the links of the chain: worship the triple Fire: knowledge, meditation, practice; the triple process: evidence, inference, experience; the triple duty: study, concentration, renunciation; understand that everything comes from Spirit, that Spirit alone is sought and found; attain everlasting peace; mount beyond birth and death.

When man understands himself, understands universal Self, the union of the two, kindles the triple Fire, offers the sacrifice; then shall he, though still on earth, break the bonds of death, beyond sorrow, mount into heaven.

This Fire that leads to heaven is your second gift, Nachiketas! It shall be named after you. Now choose again, choose the third gift.

Nachiketas said: Some say that when man dies he continues to exist, others that he does not. Explain, and that shall be my third gift.

Death said: This question has been discussed by the gods, it is deep and difficult. Choose another gift, Nachiketas! Do not be hard. Do not compel me to explain.

Nachiketas said: 'Death! you say that the gods have discussed it, that it is deep and difficult; what explanation can be as good as yours? What gift compares with that?

Death said: Take sons and grandsons, all long-lived, cattle and horses, elephants and gold, take a great kingdom.

Anything but this; wealth, long life, Nachiketas! empire, anything whatever; satisfy the heart's desire.

Pleasures beyond human reach, fine women with carriages, their musical instruments; mount beyond dreams; enjoy. But do not ask what lies beyond death.

Nachiketas said: Destroyer of man! these things pass. Joy ends enjoyment, the longest life is short. Keep those horses, keep singing and dancing, keep it all for yourself.

Wealth cannot satisfy a man. If he but please you, Master of All, he can live as long as he likes, get all that he likes; but I will not change my gift.

What man, subject to death and decay, getting the chance of undecaying life, would still enjoy mere long life, thinking of copulation and beauty.

Say where man goes after death; end all that discussion. This, which you have made so mysterious, is the only gift I will take.

2

Death said: 'The good is one, the pleasant another; both command the soul. Who follows the good, attains sanctity ; who follows the pleasant, drops out of the race.

Every man faces both. The mind of the wise man draws him to the good, the flesh of the fool drives him to the pleasant.

Nachiketas! Having examined the pleasures you have rejected them; turned from the vortex of life and death.

Diverging roads: one called ignorance, the other wisdom. Rejecting images of pleasure, Nachiketas! you turn towards wisdom.

Fools brag of their knowledge; proud, ignorant, dissolving, blind led by the blind, staggering to and fro.

What can the money-maddened simpleton know of the future? "This is the only world" cries he; because he thinks there is no other I kill him again and again.

Some have never heard of the Self, some have heard but cannot find Him. Who finds Him is a world's wonder, who expounds Him is a world's wonder, who inherits Him from his Master is a world's wonder.

No man of common mind can teach Him; such men dispute one against another. But when the uncommon man speaks, dispute is over. Because the Self is a fine substance, He slips from the mind and deludes imagination.

Beloved! Logic brings no man to the Self. Yet when a wise man shows Him, He is found. Your longing eyes are turned towards reality. Would that I had always such a pupil.

Because man cannot find the Eternal through passing pleasure, I have sought the Fire in these pleasures and, worshipping that alone, found the Eternal.

Nachiketas! The fulfillment of all desire, the conquest of the world, freedom from fear, unlimited pleasure, magical power, all were yours, but you renounced them all, brave and wise man.

The wise, meditating on God, concentrating their thought, discovering in the mouth of the cavern, deeper in the cavern, that Self, that ancient Self, difficult to imagine, more difficult to understand, pass beyond joy and sorrow.

The man that, hearing from the Teacher and comprehending, distinguishes nature from the Self, goes to the source; that man attains joy, lives forever in that joy. I think, Nachiketas! your gates of joy stand open.

Nachiketas asked: What lies beyond right and wrong, beyond cause and effect, beyond past and future?

Death said: The word the Wedas extol, austerities proclaim, sanctities approach—that word is Om. [Spelt AUM, pronounced as 'oam' in 'foam']

That word is eternal Spirit, eternal distance; who knows it attains to his desire.

That word is the ultimate foundation. Who finds it is adored among the saints.

The Self knows all, is not born, does not die, is not the effect of any cause; is eternal, self-existent, imperishable, ancient. How can the killing of the body kill Him?

He who thinks that He kills, he who thinks that He is killed, is ignorant. He does not kill nor is He killed.

The Self is lesser than the least, greater than the greatest. He lives in all hearts. When senses are at rest, free from desire, man finds Him and mounts beyond sorrow.

Though sitting, He travels; though sleeping is everywhere. Who but I Death can understand that God is beyond joy and sorrow.

Who knows the Self, bodiless among the embodied, unchanging among the changing, prevalent everywhere, goes beyond sorrow.

The Self is not known through discourse, splitting of hairs, learning however great; He comes to the man He loves; takes that man's body for His own.

The wicked man is restless, without concentration, without peace; how can he find Him, whatever his learning?

He has made mere preachers and soldiers His food, death its condiment; how can a common man find Him?

The individual self and the universal Self, living in the heart, like shade and light, though beyond enjoyment, enjoy the result of action. All say this, all who know Spirit, whether householder or ascetic.

Man can kindle that Fire, that Spirit, a bridge for all who sacrifice, a guide for all who pass beyond fear.

Self rides in the chariot of the body, intellect the firm-footed charioteer, discursive mind the reins.

Senses are the horses, objects of desire the roads. When Self is joined to body, mind, sense, none but He enjoys.

When a man lack steadiness, unable to control his mind, his senses are unmanageable horses.

But if he control his mind, a steady man, they are manageable horses.

The impure, self-willed, unsteady man misses the goal and is born again and again.

The self-controlled, steady, pure man goes to that goal from which he never returns.

He who calls intellect to manage the reins of his mind reaches the end of his journey, finds there all-pervading Spirit.

Above the senses are the objects of desire, above the objects of desire mind, above the mind intellect, above the intellect manifest nature.

Above manifest nature the unmanifest seed, above the unmanifest seed, God. God is the goal; beyond Him nothing.

God does not proclaim Himself, He is everybody's secret, but the intellect of the sage has found Him.

The wise man would lose his speech in mind, mind in the intellect, intellect in nature, nature in God and so find peace.

Get up! Stir yourself! Learn wisdom at the Master's feet. A hard path the sages say, the sharp edge of a razor.

He who knows the soundless, odourless, tasteless, intangible, formless, deathless, supernatural, undecaying, beginningless, endless, unchangeable Reality, springs out of the mouth of Death.

Those who hear and repeat correctly this ancient dialogue between Death and Nachiketas are approved by holy men.

He who sings this great mystery at the anniversary of his fathers to a rightly chosen company, finds good luck, good luck beyond measure.

Book II

1

Death said: God made sense turn outward, man therefore looks outward, not into himself. Now and again a daring soul, desiring immortality, has looked back and found himself.

The ignorant man runs after pleasure, sinks into the entanglements of death; but the wise man, seeking the undying, does not run among things that die.

He through whom we see, taste, smell, feel, hear, enjoy, knows everything. He is that Self.

The wise man by meditating upon the self-dependent, all-pervading Self, understands waking and sleeping and goes beyond sorrow.

Knowing that the individual self, eater of the fruit of action, is the universal Self, maker of past and future, he knows he has nothing to fear.

He knows that He himself born in the beginning out of meditation, before water was created, enters every heart and lives there among the elements.

That boundless Power, source of every power, manifesting itself as life, entering every heart, living there among the elements, that is Self.

The Fire, hidden in the fire-stick like a child in the womb, worshipped with offerings, that Fire is Self.

He who makes the sun rise and set, to Whom all powers do homage, He that has no master, that is Self.

That which is here, is hereafter ; hereafter is here. He who thinks otherwise wanders from death to death.

Tell the mind that there is but One; he who divides the One, wanders from death to death.

When that Person in the heart, no bigger than a thumb, is known as maker of past and future, what more is there to fear? That is Self.

That Person, no bigger than a thumb, burning like flame without smoke, maker of past and future, the same today and tomorrow, that is Self.

As rain upon a mountain ridge runs down the slope, the man that has seen the shapes of Self runs after them everywhere.

The Self of the wise man remains pure; pure water, Nachiketas, poured into pure water.

2

Who meditates on self-existent, pure intelligence, ruler of the body, the city of eleven gates, grieves no more, is free, forever free.

He is sun in the sky, fire upon the altar, guest in the house, air that runs everywhere, Lord of lords, living in reality. He abounds everywhere, is renewed in the sacrifice, born in water, springs out of the soil, breaks out of the mountain; power: reality.

Living at the centre, adorable, adored by the senses, He breathes out, breathes in.

When He, the bodiless, leaves the body, exhausts the body, what leaves? That is Self.

Man lives by more than breath; he lives by the help of another who makes it come and go.

Nachiketas! I will tell you the secret of undying Spirit and what happens after death.

Some enter the womb, waiting for a moving body, some pass into unmoving things: according to deed and knowledge.

Who is awake, who creates lovely dreams, when man is lost in sleep? That Person through whom all things live, beyond whom none can go; pure, powerful, immortal Spirit.

As fire, though one, takes the shape of whatsoever it consumes, so the Self, though one, animating all things, takes the shape of whatsoever it animate; yet stands outside.

As air, though one, takes the shape of whatsoever it enters, so the Self, though one, animating all things, takes the shape of whatsoever it animates; yet stands outside.

As the sun, the eye of the world, is not touched by the impurity it looks upon, so the Self, though one, animating all things, is not moved by human misery but stands outside.

He is One, Governor, Self of all, Creator of many out of one. He that dare discover Him within, rejoices; what other dare rejoice?

He is imperishable among things that perish. Life of all life, He, though one, satisfies every man's desire. He that dare discover Him within, knows peace; what other dare know peace?'

Nachiketas asked: Where shall I find that joy beyond all words? Does He reflect another's light or shine of Himself?

Death replied: Neither sun, moon, stars, fire nor lightning lights Him. When He shines, everything begins to shine. Everything in the world reflects His light.

4

Eternal creation is a tree, with roots above, branches on the ground; pure eternal Spirit, living in all things and beyond whom none can go; that is Self.

Everything owes life and movement to Spirit. Spirit strikes terror, hangs like a thunderbolt overhead; find it, find immortality.

Through terror of God fire burns, sun shines, rain pours, wind blows, death speeds.

Man, if he fail to find Him before the body falls, must take another body.

Man, looking into the mirror of himself may know Spirit there as he knows light from shade; but in the world of spirits It is known distorted as in a dream, in the choir of angels as though reflected on troubled water.

He who knows that the senses belong not to Spirit but to the elements, that they are born and die, grieves no more.

Mind is above sense, intellect above mind, nature above intellect, the unmanifest above nature.

Above the unmanifest is God, unconditioned, filling all things. He who finds Him enters immortal life, becomes free.

No eye can see Him, nor has He a face that can be seen, yet through meditation and through discipline He can be found in the heart. He that finds Him enters immortal life.

When mind and sense are at rest, when the discrimination of intellect is finished, man comes to his final condition.

Yoga brings the constant control of sense. When that condition is reached the Yogi can do no wrong. Before it is reached Yoga seems union and again disunion.

He cannot be known through discourse, nor found by the mind or the eye. He that believes in His existence finds Him. How can a man who does not so believe find Him?

Go backward from effect to cause until you are compelled to believe in Him. Once you are so compelled, truth dawns.

When the desires of the heart are finished, man though still in the body is united to Spirit ; mortal becomes immortal.

When the knot of the heart is cut, mortal becomes immortal. This is the law.

The heart has a hundred and one arteries; one of these—Sushumna—goes up into the head. He who climbs through it attains immortality; others drive him into the vortex.

God, the inmost Self, no bigger than a thumb, lives in the heart. Man should strip him of the body, as the arrow-maker strips the reed, that he may know Him as perpetual and pure; what can He be but perpetual and pure?

Then Nachiketas having learnt from Death this knowledge, learnt the method of meditation, rose above desire and death, found God: who does the like, finds Him.

IV

Questions

Prashna Upanishad

1

May our ears hear the good. Lords! inspiration of sacrifice! May our eyes see the good. May we serve him with the whole strength of our body. May we, all our life, carry out his will. May peace and peace and peace be everywhere.

Welcome to the Lord!

Sukesha Bharadwaja, Satyakama Shaibya, Sour-yayanee Gargya, Kousalya Ashwalayana, Bhargawa Waidarbhee and Kabandhee Katyayana, students and devotees, brought their offerings and their faith to Sage Pippalada.

The Sage said: 'Stay with me for a year, practice faith, austerity, continence; then ask what questions you like.

2

At the end of a year Kabandhee Katyayana said: 'Lord ! Who created all things?

The Sage said: The Creator, His mind's eye on the world made a couple in meditation, life and matter, thinking they would do the rest.

Sun is life, Moon matter; World moveable and immoveable is matter, all shape matter.

The sun looks into the east, then into the other quarters, then above and below, enlivening, lighting.

He, all-prevalent life, first shows himself as Light. Here is my authority:

"The wise know Him, the all pervading, all illuminating, all knowing, the One, upholder of all, and say that He rises as the sun that He may warm everything, go into everything, its particular life."

The year is the Creator. There are two paths, the southern and the northern. Those that are content with alms-giving and ritual preferring the life of the family, go to their ancestors by the southern path, attain the lunar world and are born again. All there is matter.

But those who seek the Self through austerity, continence, faith, knowledge, go by the northern path, attain the solar world. It is living, immortal, beyond fear; it is the goal. Once there, there is no return.

It is the law. Here is my authority:

"Some call the sun our protector, with five seasons or feet, twelve moons or bodies, who lives beyond the sky and sends the rain. Others call Him the year, reckoner of time, who rides in the chariot of seven colours or seven horses, and of six wheels considering that the number of seasons."

The month too is the Creator, its bright half is life, its dark half matter. Wise men perform their rituals in the bright half; fools in the dark.

The round of day and night is the Creator; day life, night matter. Those that couple with a woman by day, waste life ; those that couple by night, preserve it.

Food is the Creator. Food makes the seed; all things are from seed.

Those who obey God as Creator, get all that life and matter can give. Those who practise austerity, continence, veracity go beyond these into Heaven.

They that are neither crooked, nor hypocritical, nor lying, go beyond into pure Heaven,'

Bhargawa Waidarbnee asked: Lord! What powers have knit the body? What powers give it life? Which is the greatest?

The Sage said: The powers are: air, fire, water, earth, speech, mind, light, hearing. All these said aloud that they had knit the body.

Life, greater than these, said: you deceive yourselves. It is I alone, dividing myself into five streams, knit and enliven the body. But they would not believe.

Life, to vindicate himself, rose as though he wanted to leave the body. But as he rose, others knew that they too must rise. When he returned they returned. As bees follow their queen when she goes out; return when she returns; speech, mind, light, hearing returned: they began to praise life.

Life burns in the fire, shines in the Sun. Rain, cloud, air, earth, are life. Matter is life. All that has shape or no shape is life. Life is immortality.

Everything is fixed in life, as are spokes in the hub of a wheel—the three Wedas, all sacrifices, all soldiers, all priests.

Life, Lord of Creation, moving in the womb, there bringing yourself to birth, master of the five streams! All things offer you their tribute.

You carry the offerings to the gods and the fathers; even breath and sense your handiwork.

Life! Creator, Protector, Destroyer! Sun in heavenly circuit! Master of stars!

Pour down the rain, let all things find their food, thrive, rejoice.

Life itself! Purity itself! Fire itself, Eater, Master! All the world your food, Father in Heaven!

May your body be in our speech, hearing, sight, mind, make us lucky, and never forsake us.

May Life, Master of the three worlds, protect us as a mother protects her children. Grant us wisdom, grant us luck.

4

Kousalya Ashwalayana asked. 'Lord! when does life begin; how does it get into the body; how does it live there after dividing itself; how does it get out of the body; how does it support all that is outside, all that is inside?

The Sage said: 'You ask weighty questions; you dig into the root. Here is my answer:

Life falls from Self as shadow falls from man. Life and Self are interwoven, but Life comes into the body that the desires of the mind may be satisfied.

As the king portions out his kingdom under different officials, life portions out .the body under five living streams.

The organs of excretion and generation under the downward stream Apana ; eye, ear, where He lives himself under Prana, which passes out through mouth and nose ; the middle of the body under the equalizing stream Samana, distributor of food, kindler of the seven flames.

Self lives in the heart. There are a hundred and one arteries, from every artery start one hundred veins, from every vein seventy-two thousand smaller veins-all these He has put under the diffusing stream Wyana.

Climbing through one of these the upward stream Udana leads the meritorious man to his reward; the sinful man to his punishment; if his merit and demerit are mixed, back to the world.

Rising sun is the symbol of life; sun maintains Prana of the eye; earth draws down Apana; air, filler of all, maintains Samana; wind, Wyana.

Light maintains Udana. When that light is out, sense dissolves in mind, man is born again.

Udana united to the mind's desire at the moment of death, returns to Life, and Life, Udana lighting the way, brings the soul to whatever place it deserves.

The man who knows this, knows the meaning of life; his children are never lost. Here is my authority:

"He who knows the source and power of Life, how it enters, where it lives, how it divides itself into five, how it is related to the Self, attains immortality ; yes, attains immortality."

5

Souryayanee Gargya asked: Lord! Who in man's body wakes, sleeps, dreams, enjoys? On whom do these depend?

The Sage said: As the rays of the setting sun gather themselves up into his orb to come out again at sunrise, so the senses gather themselves up into the mind, master of them all. Therefore when a man does not hear, see, touch, smell, taste, speak, receive, give, move, enjoy, we say that he sleeps.

Only the living fires are then awake. The living fire Apana corresponds to the everlasting sacrificial Garha-patya fire of the householder; the living fire Wyana corresponds to the sacrificial Anwarhapachan fire that faces south and the southern path; the living fire Prana, lit from the fire Apana, corresponds to the sacrificial Ahawaneeya, fire lit from the everlasting Garhapatya fire that faces east and the rising sun.

The living fire Samana is called the equalising fire, because it balances those oblations, the outgoing and the incoming breath. Mind is the sacrificer. The reward of the sacrifice is the living fire Udana, the deep sleep that again and again leads mind to Self.

The dreaming mind enjoys its greatness. What it has seen it sees again; what it has heard it hears again; what it has enjoyed in different countries and climates it enjoys again. Whatever is seen, unseen, heard, unheard, enjoyed, unenjoyed, real, unreal, here and there, it knows; it knows everything.

When mind is lost in the light of the Self, it dreams no more; still in the body it is lost in that happiness.

My son! All things fly to the Self, as birds fly to the tree for rest.

Earth, its quality of scent; water, its quality of taste; light, its quality of beauty; wind, its quality of touch; air, its quality of sound; eye, what it sees; ear, what it hears; nose, what it smells; tongue, what it tastes; skin, what it touches; voice, what it says; hands, what they handle; generation, what incites it; excretion, what is excreted; feet, what they tread upon; mind, what it imagines; intellect, what it discriminates; pride, what swells it; thought, what is thought; light, what is lit; life, what depends upon it; all these fly towards the Self.

This is the Self who sees, touches, hears, smells, tastes, thinks, discriminates, acts. The personal self and the ultimate imperishable, impersonal Self, are one.

My son! Who knows the impersonal Self, wherein the personal self, the living fires, senses, elements live, he knows all; lives in all. Here is my authority:

"He who finds the imperishable Being where the individual self, sense, vitality and elements live, he knows all; pervades all."

6

Satyakama Shaibya asked: Lord! Where does the man go after his life, if he meditates on Om all his life?

The Sage said: Om is the conditioned and the unconditioned Spirit. The wise man with its help alone attains the one or the other.

If he meditates on the syllable A alone he is soon born again on this earth. If he has chanted the Rig-Weda, he is born among men, a great, austere, self-controlled, God-fearing man.

If he meditates on the two syllables A and U, and has chanted the Yajur-Weda, he goes to the moon and, after enjoying its pleasure, returns to the earth again and again.

He who meditates on the three syllables A, U, M, as upon God, is joined to the light of the sun. Peeling his evil off, as the snake peels off its skin, he goes through that light, with the help of Sama-Weda chants, to the Kingdom of Heaven, to the God greater than the greatest of all creatures though living in our body. Here is my authority;

"If man meditates on the three syllables in separation, it is the emblem of mortality; but if he meditate upon all together, insepa-

rable, interdependent, the three conditions, physical, mental, intellectual, reward him; he goes beyond mortality.

Rig-Weda brings man to earth, Yajur-Weda sends him to the sky, but only the Seer knows the world which Sama-Weda brings. The wise man with the help of Om goes there, beyond decay, death, fear; attains peace.

7

Sukesha Bharadwaja said: Lord! I was asked this question by Hiranyanabha, Prince of Koasala: *"Bharadwaja! Do you know God and his sixteen phases?"*—I said to the young man: "I do not. I will not lie about it, for I know what happens to the liar. If I did, I would tell you." The Prince mounted his chariot, and went away without a word. Now I ask: *"Where is that God?"*

The Sage said: My son, that God and his sixteen phases are in this body.

God thought to himself: *"What is that which compels me to go if it goes, to stay if it stays?"*

He then created life; from life, knowledge; from knowledge, air; from air, wind; from wind, light; from light, water; from water, earth; from earth, sense; from sense, mind; from mind, food; from food, vigor; from vigor, austerity; from austerity, revelation; from revelation, karma; from karma, world; from world, the names.

When rivers mingle with the sea they lose their names and shapes and people speak of the sea only, so these sixteen phases, when they mingle with God, lose their names and shapes and people speak of God only; man becomes the phaseless, the timeless. Here is my authority:

"*God is the hub of the wheel where the sixteen phases are the spokes, know Him and die no more.*"

What I have told you is all that is known about Spirit.

They worshipped the Sage and said: You are indeed our father. You have led us to the further shore. All bow down to you, Great Sage! Bow down to the Great Sages!

V

At the feet of the Monk
Mundaka Upanishad

Book I

1

Lords, inspiration of sacrifice! May our ears hear the good. May our eyes see the good. May we serve Him with the whole strength of our body. May we, all our life, carry out His will. May peace and peace and peace be everywhere.

The Creator came first; He created Himself as Creator then called Himself the Protector of the world. He gave the knowledge of Spirit, foundation of all knowledge, to his eldest son Atharwa.

Atharwa gave it to Angee; Angee to Satyawaha Bharadwaja; Satyawaha Bharadwaja to Angiras.

That famous man the householder Shounaka said to Angiras: "What is it that when known, makes us know everything in the world?"

Angiras said: "Those who know Spirit say that there are two kinds of knowledge, a lower and a higher.

The lower is the knowledge of the four Wedas and such things as pronunciation, ceremonial, grammar, etymology, poetry, astronomy, The higher knowledge is the knowledge of the Everlasting;

Of that which has neither tangibility, nor antecedent, colour, eyes, ears, hands, feet; of that which is prevalent everywhere, immeasurably minute, self-evident, indestructible, always alive; of that which the wise name the Source.

As the web springs from the spider and is again withdrawn, as the plant springs from the soil, hairs from the body of man, so springs the world from the Everlasting.

Brooding Spirit creates food, food life, life mind, mind the elements, the elements the world, the world Karma, Karma the Everlasting.

He looks at all things; knows all things. All things, their nourishment, their names, their forms, are from His will, All that He has willed is right.

2

The Sages studied the rituals described in the Wedas, went beyond them to the truth. You may find it better to stay with them; if you seek the reward of your actions, stay with them.

When the sacrificial fire has been kindled, set it ablaze with butter, pour an oblation, then let the butter set it ablaze again.

If the worshipper does not offer his sacrifice, according to the rules, during the new moon, or full moon, or at the rainy season, or at harvest time, if he offer it without regularity or at other seasons, or not at all, if he entertain no guests at the sacrifice, his people for seven generations shall be unlucky.

There are seven tongues of fire, the ruinous, the terrible, the swift, the smoky, the red, the bright, the flickering.

If the sacrifice has been made at the right time, the tongues, emblem of the solar rays, carry the devotee into paradise.

'Welcome! Welcome!' cry his pleasant flattering good deeds, as the tongues, emblem of the solar rays, carry him. 'Look upon what we have made for you, look upon this beautiful paradise.'

Those sacrifices with their crew of eighteen men, are unseaworthy ships, belong to a trivial karma. The fool fixes his hopes upon them; goes to wreck.

Fools brag of their knowledge, proud, ignorant, dissolving; staggering to and fro, blind and led by the blind;

Dunces think, in their pride, that they have solved every problem; the passionate never learn. All these, the merit of their sacrifice exhausted, are thrust from paradise into the misery of life.

These dunces think ritual and alms are enough, they know nothing of the good itself; when ritual and alms have done their work, they fall into their old human life or it may be lower still.

The wise and the clean, content with what they get, living in solitude, practicing austerities, go to the Deathless, through the gates of the sun.

He that understands the results of action, wants to renounce them all. Activity cannot attain the Inactive; therefore, with hands folded, let him go to some teacher who lives in Spirit and in whom revelation lives.

To such a pupil, humble, master of mind and sense, the teacher can teach all he knows, bringing him to the Deathless.

Book II

1

This is the truth: the sparks, though of one nature with the fire, leap from it; uncounted beings leap from the Everlasting, but these, my son, merge into It again.

The Everlasting is shapeless, birthless, breathless, mindless, above everything, outside everything, inside everything.

From Him are born life, mind, sense, air, wind, water, earth that supports all.

He is the inmost Self of all. Fire, His head; sun and moon, His eyes; the four quarters, His ears; revelation, His voice; wind, His breath; world, His heart; earth, His feet.

Fire is from Him, its fuel sun, moon from sun, rain from moon, food from rain, man from food, seed from man; thus all descends from God.

From Him are hymns, holy chants, ritual, initiation, sacrifice, ceremonial, oblation, time, deeds, everything under sun and moon;

From Him, gods, angels, men, cattle, birds, living fires, rice, barley, austerity, faith, truth, continence, law;

From Him seven senses like ritual fires, seven desires like flames, seven objects like oblations, seven pleasures like sacrifices, seven nerves like habitations, seven centres in the heart like hollows in the cavern.

From Him, seas, rivers, mountains, herbs and their properties: in the middle of the elements the inmost Self.

My son! There is nothing in this world that is not God, He is action, purity; everlasting Spirit, Find Him in the cavern; gnaw the knot of ignorance.

2

Shining, yet hidden, Spirit lives in the cavern. Everything that sways, breathes, opens, closes, lives in Spirit; beyond learning, beyond everything, better than anything; living, unliving.

It is the undying blazing Spirit, that seed of all seeds, wherein lay hidden the world and all its creatures. It is life, speech, mind, reality, immortality. It is there to be struck. Strike it, my son!

Take the bow of our sacred knowledge, lay against it the arrow of devotion, pull the string of concentration, strike the target.

Om is the bow, the personal self the arrow, impersonal Self the target. Aim accurately, sink therein.

Into His cloak are woven earth, mind, life, the canopy, the Kingdom of Heaven. He is alone and sole; man's bridge to immortality.

Come out of all the schools. Meditate upon Om as the Self. Remember He takes many shapes, lives in the hub where the arteries meet; and may His blessing bring you out of the darkness.

He knows all, knows every particular. His glory prevails on earth, in heaven, in His own seat, the holy city of the heart.

He becomes mind and guides body and life. He lives in man's heart and eats man's food. He that knows Him, in finding joy, finds immortality.

He that knows Him as the shaped and the shapeless, cuts through the knot of his heart, solves every doubt, exhausts every action.

In a beautiful golden scabbard hides the stainless, indivisible, luminous Spirit.

Neither sun, moon, star, neither fire nor lightning, lights Him. When He shines, everything begins to shine. Everything in the world reflects His light.

Spirit is everywhere, upon the right, upon the left, above, below, behind, in front. What is the world but Spirit?

Book III

1

Two birds, bound one to another in friendship, have made their homes on the same tree. One stares about him, one pecks at the sweet fruit.

The personal self, weary of pecking here and there, sinks into dejection; but when he understands through meditation that the other—the impersonal Self—is indeed Spirit, dejection disappears.

When the sage meets Spirit, phallus and what it enters, good and evil disappear, they are one.

The sage who knows Him as life and the giver of life, does not assert himself; playing with Self, enjoying Self, doing his duty, he takes his rank.

The Self is found by veracity, purity, intelligence, continence. The ascetic, so purged, discovers His burning light in the heart.

Falsehood turns from the way; truth goes all the way; the end of the way is truth; the way is paved with truth. The sage travels there without desire.

Truth lies beyond imagination, beyond paradise; great, smaller than the smallest; near, further than the furthest; hiding from the traveler in the cavern.

Nor can penance discover Him, nor ritual reveal, nor eye see, nor tongue speak; only in meditation can mind, grown pure and still, discover formless truth.

The Self shines out of the pure heart, when life enters with its five fires and fills the mind.

A pure man gets all he wants. A man with mind fixed upon some man who knows the Self, gets all he wants.

2

The daring man adores the knower of that Spirit, wherein the world lives and is bright; knows him escaped from the seminal fluid.

He who desires one thing after another, brooding over them, is born where his desires can be satisfied; but the Self attained, one desire satisfied, all are satisfied.

The Self is not known through discourse, splitting of hairs, learning however great. He comes to the man He loves; takes that man's body as His own.

Blunderers, charlatans, weaklings, cannot attain the Self. He is found by the pure, daring, cautious man.

He who has found Him, seeks no more; the riddle is solved; desire gone, he is at peace. Having approached from everywhere that which is everywhere, whole, he passes into the Whole.

When the ascetic has mastered theory and practice, he forgets body, remembers Spirit, attains immortality.

His phases return to their source, his senses to their gods, his personal self and all his actions to the impersonal imperishable Self.

As rivers lose name and shape in the sea, wise men lose name and shape in God, glittering beyond all distance.

He who has found Spirit, is Spirit. Nobody ignorant of Spirit is born into his family. He goes beyond sorrow, sin, death; the knots of his heart unloosed.

The Rig-Weda says 'Tell this to those that know the Wedas, do their duty, obey the law, make themselves an oblation to the sole Fire.'

This is that ancient Truth," sage Angiras declared. "Obey the law and understand"

We bow down to you, Great Sage!

Bow down to you, Great Sages!

VI
At The Feet Of Master Mandooka
Mandookya Upanishad

Lords! inspiration of sacrifice!

May our ears hear the good.

May our eyes see the good.

May we serve Him with the whole strength of our body.

May we, all our life, carry out His will.

Peace, peace, and peace be everywhere.

Welcome to the Lord!

The word Om is the Imperishable ; all this its manifestation. Past, present, future—everything is Om. Whatever transcends the three divisions of time, that too is Om.

There is nothing that is not Spirit. The personal self is the impersonal Spirit. It has four conditions.

First comes the material condition—common to all —perception turned outward, seven agents [*Heavens (head), sun (eye), air (breath), fire (heart), water (belly), earth (feet), and space (body)*] nineteen agencies [*Five organs of sense—hearing, touching, seeing, tasting and smelling; five organs of action—speaking, handling, walking, generating and excreting; five living fires—Prana, Apana, Wyana, Udana and Samana; Discursive mind (Manas), Discriminative mind (Buddhi), Mind-Material (Chitta) and Personality (Ahangkara)*] wherein the Self enjoys coarse matter. This is known as the waking condition.

The second is the mental condition, perception turned inward, seven agents, nineteen agencies, wherein the Self enjoys subtle matter. This is known as the dreaming condition.

In deep sleep man feels no desire, creates no dream. This undreaming sleep is the third condition, the intellectual condition. Because of his union with the Self and his unbroken knowledge of it, he is filled with joy, he knows his joy; his mind is illuminated.

The Self is the lord of all; inhabitant of the hearts of all. He is the source of all; creator and dissolver of beings. There is nothing He does not know.

He is not knowable by perception, turned inward or outward, nor by both combined. He is neither that which is known, nor that which is not known, nor is He the sum of all that might be known. He cannot be seen, grasped, bargained with. He is undefinable, unthinkable, indescribable.

The only proof of His existence is union with Him. The world disappears in Him. He is the peaceful, the good, the one without a second. This is the fourth condition of the Self—the most worthy of all. This Self, though beyond words, is that supreme word Om; though indivisible, it can be divided in three letters corresponding to the three conditions of the Self, the letter A [*'A' is pronounced short like the sound of V in 'her', 'U' as in 'put', and 'M' as 'Me' in 'Merchant'*], the letter U, and the letter M.

The waking-condition, called the material condition, corresponds to the letter A, which leads the alphabet and breathes in all the other letters. He who understands, gets all he wants ; becomes a leader among men.

The dreaming condition, called the mental condition, corresponds to the second letter U. It upholds; stands between waking and sleeping. He who understands, upholds the tradition of spiritual knowledge 5 looks upon everything with an impartial eye. No one ignorant of Spirit is born into his family.

Undreaming sleep, called the intellectual condition, corresponds to the third letter, M. It weighs and unites. He who understands, weighs the world; rejects; unites himself with the cause.

The fourth condition of the Self corresponds to Om as One, indivisible Word. He is whole; beyond bargain. The world disappears in Him. He is the good; the one without a second. Thus Om is nothing but Self. He who understands, with the help of his personal self, merges himself into the impersonal Self; He who understands.

VII

From The Taittireeya Branch Of the Wedas

Taittireeya Upanishad

Book I

Admonition

1

May the Sun bless us! May the Night bless us! May the Eye bless us! May Might bless us! May Speech bless us! May the All-prevalent bless us! Welcome Spirit! Welcome Life, Face of Spirit! Truth shall be on my lips and truth in my thoughts. May truth protect me; protect my teacher; protect us both. May peace and peace and peace be everywhere.

2

We explain what constitutes pronunciation. It comprises letters, accent, quantity, articulation, rhythm, and lastly sequence of letters.

3

Grant success! Grant that we may be one in the light of Spirit!

This chapter deals with the world, heavenly bodies, education, generation, language.

What is this world? Earth below, heaven above, air between, wind joining them.

What are the heavenly bodies? Fire on one side, sun on the other side, water between, lightning joining them.

What is education? The teacher on one side, pupil on the other side, knowledge between, discourse joining them.

What is generation? Mother on one side, father on the other side, child between, procreation joining them.

What is language? The lower jaw on one side, the upper jaw on the other side, words between, tongue joining them.

This is the summary. He who knows them all, shall have children, cattle, food, knowledge, heaven.

4

Om! Essence of the Wedas, revealed in the Wedas, revealed in the world, sprung from immortality! Lord, fill me with intelligence, that I may grasp immortality!

Make my body strong, my tongue sweet, my ears keen. You are the Spirit's armour, hidden by sensuality. Keep me from forgetting.

May spiritual riches come of their own will. May they increase, then send me Spirit itself. May I never lack clothes, cows, food, drink, that I may serve you the better. May pupils come, may pupils gather round, may pupils listen, that I may serve you the better. May they in peace, control mind and sense, that they may serve you the better.

May I become famous, may I become richer than the richest, that I may serve you the better.

Lord! may I enter into you, may you enter into me! may I merge into your thousands of shapes, for my purification.

As water flows downward, as months mingle with the year, Guardian! may pupils come from everywhere, that I may serve you the better.

You are the Fold. Take me. Enlighten me.

5

Bhoohu, Bhuwaha, Suwaha, are sacred sounds. Sage Mahachamasya taught a fourth, Mahes, meaning Spirit, meaning God. The others are His limbs.

When Bhoohu is earth, Bhuwaha sky, Suwaha heaven, Mahas is the sun; for everything is sustained by the sun.

When Bhoohu is fire, Bhuwaha wind, Suwaha sun, Mahas is the moon; for planets are sustained by the moon.

When Bhoohu is Rig-Weda, Bhuwaha Sama-Weda, Suwaha Yajur-Weda, Mahas is Spirit; for the Wedas are sustained by Spirit.

When Bhoohu is Prana, Bhuwaha Apana, Suwaha VVyana, Mahas is Food; for the living fires are sustained by food.

Thus there are four times four, sixteen sacred sounds. He who knows them, knows Spirit; all gods will pay him homage.

6

God lives in the hollow of the heart, filling it with immortality, light, intelligence.

Where the skull divides and where it is customary to divide the hair, lies the hollow, where the gate of God swings, like the uvula within the palate.

Through that gate man goes forth into fire crying Bhoohu, into air crying Bhuwaha, into sun crying Suwaha, into Spirit crying Mahas.

In Spirit, he attains heaven, conquers his mind; becomes master of speech, sight, hearing, knowledge.

He becomes Spirit itself, which has for its body air, for its soul truth, for its rest life; there he is peaceful, merry, immortal.

Worship Spirit, now that you are fit to worship ancient Spirit.

7

Earth, sky, heavens, quarters, sub-quarters; fire, wind, sun, moon, stars; water, air, herb, food, body; are elements.

Prana, Wyana, Apana, Udana, Samana; eye, ear, mind, tongue, touch; skin, flesh, muscle, bone, marrow; are the body.

A Sage said, understanding these sets of five: *Everything is sacred; for with the help of the latter, man conquers the former.*

8

Om is Spirit. Everything is but 6m.

Om permits, Om gives the signal. Om begins the ceremony. All chants begin with Om. All hymns begin with Om. The priest begins with Om. His commands are in the name of Om. The sacrificer offers the oblation with Om. The teacher begins with Om. The pupil begins with Om,

The pupil murmuring Om seeks for Spirit; in the end he finds Spirit.

9

Do your duty; learn and teach. Speak truth; learn and teach. Meditate; learn and teach. Control sense; learn and teach. Control mind; learn and teach. Kindle fire; learn and teach. Feed fire; learn and teach. Be hospitable; learn and teach. Be humane; learn and teach. Serve the family; learn and teach. Procreate; learn and teach. Educate your children; learn and teach.

Ratheetara Satyawacha says: *Truth is necessary*. Paurushishti Taponitya says: *Austerity is necessary*. Moudgalya Naka says: *Learning and teaching are necessary*.

Learning and teaching, they are austerity; they are austerity.

10

I nourish the tree of life.

My glory is like the mountain peak.

I am exalted, wise, luminous, immortal, pure.

I am the life that flows from the sun.

So said sage Trishanku, having attained.

After teaching the Wedas, teacher says to pupil: 'Speak the truth. Do your duty. Study the Wedas. Give what is fitting to the teacher; marry, continue the family. Neither neglect your spiritual nor your worldly welfare. Always learn and teach. Forget neither God nor ancestor. Your mother your goddess, your father your God, your guest your God, your teacher your God; copy our good deeds alone, so escape blame.

Look for men greater than us, welcome them, give them hospitality.

Give with faith; if you lack faith, give nothing. Give in proportion to your means. Give with courtesy. Give as the God-fearing give. Give to the deserving.

If you do not know what to do in some particular case or in your general conduct, think of what sense of duty, what kindness, independence of public opinion, some holy men of your neighbourhood, whether of an order or not, would show in like circumstance; if you do not know what to think about a man think what some such holy man would think about him.

This is the admonition, the advice, the law of the Wedas. Obey! Obey.

Book II

Joy

May He protect us both.

May He take pleasure in us both.

May we show courage together.

May Spiritual knowledge shine before us.

May we never hate one another.

May peace and peace and peace be everywhere.

1

He who knows Spirit knows the foundation. Here is my authority: He who knows Spirit as that boundless wise reality, hidden in the heart's cavern, gets all that he wants.

Out of Spirit came air, out of air, wind; out of wind, fire; out of fire, water; out of water, earth; out of earth, vegetation; out of vegetation, food; out of food, man;

Man's elemental Self comes from food: this his head; this his right arm; this his left arm; this his heart; these legs his foundation. Here is my authority:

2

From food are born all creatures; they live upon food, they are dissolved in food. Food is the chief of all things, the universal medicine.

They who think of food as Spirit, shall never lack. From food all beings are born, all beings increase their bulk; all beings feed upon it, it feeds upon all beings.

The elemental Self is from food, but within it lives its complement and completion, the living Self. The living Self grows up side by side with the elemental Self. Prana is its head, Wyana its right arm, Apana its left arm, air its heart, earth its foundation. Here is my authority:

3

Gods, men, beasts, live by breath. Breath is life and is called the giver of Life.

The living Self is the soul of the elemental Self, but within it lives its complement and completion, the thinking Self. The thinking Self grows up side by side with the living Self. Meditation is its head, ritual its right arm, prayer its left arm, admonition of the Wedas its heart, Sage Atharwangiras its foundation. Here is my authority:

4

He who knows the spiritual joy mind cannot grasp nor tongue speak, fears nothing.

The thinking Self is the soul of the living Self, but within it lives its complement and completion, the knowing Self. The knowing Self grows up side by side with the thinking Self. Faith is its head, right its right arm, truth its left arm, concentration its heart, discrimination its foundation. Here is my authority:

5

Knowledge runs to sacrifice and incites action. Gods worship knowledge as the highest expression of Spirit. The steadfast worshipper of Spirit, as knowledge, goes beyond all evil, gets everything he Wants.

The knowing Self is the soul of the thinking Self, but within it lives its complement and completion, the joyous Self. The joyous Self grows up side by side with the knowing Self. Satisfied desire is its head, pleasure its right arm, contentment its left arm, joy its heart, Spirit its foundation. Here is my authority:

6

He who denies Spirit, denies himself; he who affirms it, affirms himself.'

This joyous Self is the soul of the knowing Self.

Does an ignorant man attain Spirit after death or only a wise man?

7

God thought: 'I would be many; I will procreate.' And in the heat of his meditation created everything; creating everything He entered into everything; entering into everything He took shape yet remained shapeless; took limits yet remained limitless; made his home, yet remained homeless; created knowledge and ignorance; reality, unreality; became everything; therefore everything is reality.

Here is my authority:

In the beginning there was no creation; then creation came. He created Himself, out of Himself.

Hence He is called Self-Creator.

Everything is Self-created. He is that essence. Drinking that essence, man rejoices. If man did not lose himself in that joy, he could not breathe} he could not live. Self is the sole giver of joy.

When man finds invisible, nameless, homeless, shapeless, invulnerable rock, he is no longer terrified. To doubt Spirit is to live in terror. For that man, thinking himself wise, who doubts Spirit, Spirit becomes terror itself.

Here is my authority:

Through terror of God, sun shines, rain pours, fire burns, wind blows, death speeds.

8

What is joy?

Think of a young man, well read, ambitious, firm, strong, noble; give him all the wealth of the world, call him one unit of human joy.

Multiply that joy a hundred times, and call it one unit of the joy of those brought to the celestial choir by their good deeds. A man full of revelation, but without desire, has equal joy.

Multiply that joy a hundred times, and call it one unit of the joy of choir-born spirits, A man full of revelation, but without desire, has equal joy.

Multiply that joy a hundred times, and call it one unit of the joy of the fathers, living in their eternal paradise. A man full of revelation, but without desire, has equal joy.

Multiply that joy a hundred times, and call it one unit of the joy of heaven-born gods. A man full of revelation, but without desire, has equal joy.

Multiply that joy a hundred times, and call it one unit of the joy of gods brought to godhead by their good deeds. A man full of revelation, but without desire, has equal joy.

Multiply that joy a hundred times, and call it one unit of the joy of ruling gods. A man full of revelation, but without desire, has equal joy.

Multiply that joy a hundred times, and call it one unit of the joy of Indra, god of Power. A man full of revelation, but without desire, has equal joy.

Multiply that joy a hundred times, and call it one unit of the joy of Brihaspati, who has taught the gods. A man full of revelation, but without desire, has equal joy.

Multiply that joy a hundred times, and call it one unit of the joy of Prajapati, maker of gods. A man full of revelation, but without desire, has equal joy.

Multiply that joy a hundred times, and call it one unit of the joy of Spirit. A man full of revelation, but without desire, has equal joy.

He who lives in man, He who lives in the sun, are one.

He who knows this, cries goodbye to the world and goes beyond elemental Self, living Self, thinking Self, knowing Self, joyous Self. Here is my authority:

9

He who knows the spiritual joy mind cannot grasp nor tongue speak, fears nothing.

Should he do wrong, or leave good undone, he knows no remorse. What he does, what he does not, is sanctified; what he does not, what he does, is sanctified.

Book III

Bhrigu

May He protect us both.

May He take pleasure in us both.

May we show courage together. May spiritual knowledge shine before us.

May we never hate one another.

May peace and peace and peace be everywhere.

1

Bhrigu, seeking his father Waruna, said: "Lord! what is Spirit?"

Waruna said: "First know food, life, seeing, hearing, speaking, thinking; then that Spirit from whom all things are born, by whom they live, towards whom they move, into whom they return."

2

Bhrigu meditated and found that food is Spirit. From food all things are born, by food they live, towards food they move, into food they return.

Having found this he said to his father: "Lord! Tell me more about Spirit."

Waruna said: "Find Spirit through meditation; meditation is Spirit."

3

Bhrigu meditated and found that life is Spirit. From life all things are born, by life they live, towards life they move, into life they return.

Having found this he said to his father: "Lord! Tell me more about Spirit."

Waruna said: 'Find Spirit through meditation, meditation is Spirit."

4

Bhrigu meditated and found that mind is Spirit. From mind all things are born, by mind they live, towards mind they move, into mind they return.

Having found this he said to his father: "Lord! Tell me more about Spirit."

Waruna said: "Find Spirit through meditation; meditation is Spirit."

5

Bhrigu meditated and found that knowledge is Spirit. From knowledge all things are born, by knowledge they live, towards knowledge they move, into knowledge they return.

Having found this he said to his father: "Lord! Tell me more about Spirit."

Waruna said: "Find Spirit through meditation; meditation is Spirit."

6

Bhrigu meditated and found that joy is Spirit. From joy all things are born, by joy they live, toward joy they move, into joy they return.

This is what Bhrigu, son of Waruna, found in the hollow of his heart.

He who knows it stands on a rock; commands everything, enjoys everything; founds a family, gathers flocks and herds; grows famous through the light of Spirit; is a great man,

7

Respect food. Life is food; body lives on food. Body is life; life is body; they are food to one another.

He who knows it stands on a rock; commands everything, enjoys everything; founds a family, gathers flocks and herds; grows famous through the light of Spirit; is a great man.

8

Do not steal food. Water is food; light lives on water. Water is light; light is water; they are food for one another.

He who knows it stands on a rock; commands everything, enjoys everything; founds a family, gathers flocks and herds; grows famous through the light of Spirit; is a great man.

9

Store food. Earth is food; air lives on earth. Earth is air; air is earth; they are food for one another.

He who knows it stands on a rock; commands everything, enjoys everything; founds a family, gathers flocks and herds; grows famous through the light of Spirit; is a great man.

10

Never turn anyone from the door; gather enough food, say to the stranger: "Sir, the dinner is served." He who gives with purity, gets purity in return; he who gives with passion, gets passion in return; he who gives with ignorance, gets ignorance in return.

He who knows, meditates upon Spirit as the blessedness of speech; as Prana and Apana, the getting and giving of the two breaths; as the activity of hands, as movement of feet, as the evacuation of the bowels.

These are the customary meditations upon the body. He meditates upon Spirit as nourishment in rain, as violence in lightning, as abundance in cattle, as light in stars, as creation, joy, immortality in sex, as all-filling, all-containing nature in air.

These are the customary meditations on Nature. Worship Spirit as the support, be supported; worship Spirit as the great, become great; worship Spirit as the mind, become mind.

Bow down to Spirit as the sole object of desire, be the goal of all desire; worship Spirit as the master of all, become the master of all.

Worship Spirit as the destroyer, your enemies whether public or in your own house shall be destroyed.

He who lives in man, He who lives in the sun, are the same.

He who knows this, says goodbye to the world: goes beyond elemental Self, living Self, thinking Self, knowing Self, joyous Self.

He moves at will throughout the world, enjoying whatever he will, creating whatever shape he will, praising the unity of Spirit—miraculous, miraculous, miraculous.

I am the food, I am the food, I am the food; I am the eater, I am the eater, I am the eater; I am the link between, I am the link between, I am the link between.

I am the first among the visible and the invisible. I existed before the gods. I am the navel of immortality. Who gives me, protects me. I am food; who refuses to give me, I eat as food.

I am this world and I eat this world. Who knows this, knows.

VIII

At The Feet Of Master Aitareya

Aitareya Upanishad

1

May God be revealed; speech merge in mind; mind merge in speech.

May they bring me the Wedas.

May I ponder over that knowledge day and night, may I never forget it. Truth shall be on my lips, and truth in my thoughts.

May truth protect me; protect my teacher; protect us both.

May peace and peace and peace be everywhere.

2

There was in the beginning one sole Self; no eye winked. He thought: "Shall I create territories?"

He created territories: that of the first water, that of light, that of earth, that of water. Heaven and beyond heaven is that of the first water; sky is that of light; this mortal territory is that of earth; under earth is that of water. He thought again: "The territories are there; let me create their rulers." Out of water he lifted an egg - He warmed it, and because of His warmth a being with a mouth appeared through a crack, for His own form lay within it. From the mouth came speech; from speech fire. A nose appeared;

from its nostrils came breath, from breath air. The eyes appeared; from the eyes came sight; from sight the sun. The ears appeared; from the ears came hearing; from hearing the four quarters. The skin appeared; from the skin came hair; from hair vegetation. The heart appeared; from the heart came the mind; from the mind came the moon. The navel appeared; from the navel came the downward breath Apana; from Apana death. Sex appeared; from sex came seed; from seed water.

3

When these gods were created, they went back into the waters. Then He endowed that being with hunger and thirst. Then the gods said: "Give us some place where we can live and eat."

He created a bull out of the waters. They said: "No; it is not sufficient." He created a horse. They said: "No; it is not sufficient."

He created a man. They said: "You have done well." Because they were satisfied, man is the chief of creatures. He said to the gods: "Take your places."

Fire in the character of speech entered the mouth; air in the character of scent entered the nose; sun in the character of sight entered the eyes; four quarters in the character of hearing entered the ears; vegetation in the character of hair entered the skin; moon in the character of mind entered the heart; death in the character of Apana entered the navel; water in the character of seed entered the loins.

Hunger and thirst said; "Where is our place?" He said: "Take your place beside all the gods, for I have made you the partners of all. To whatever god man makes oblation, hunger and thirst shall partake."

He thought: "Here are the territories and their rulers. I will create food."

He meditated on water, and from the heat of meditation came an image. That image is food.

Food fled from man. Man tried to grasp it with speech but failed; had he succeeded, to talk about it had been satisfaction enough.

He tried to grasp it with breath but failed; had he succeeded, to inhale it had been satisfaction enough.

He tried to grasp it with his eyes but failed; had he succeeded, to look upon it had been satisfaction enough.

He tried to grasp it with his ears but failed; had he succeeded, to hear it had been satisfaction enough.

He tried to grasp it with his skin but failed; had he succeeded, to touch it had been satisfaction enough.

He tried to grasp it with his mind but failed; had he succeeded, thinking of it had been satisfaction enough.

He tried to grasp it with the downward breath Apana and succeeded. Apana alone receives food; Apana lives on food.

God thought: "Can they live without me? How shall I enter the body?" He knew that even if tongue spoke, breath breathed, eyes saw, ears heard, skin touched, mind thought, Apana drew in, sex threw out, they would not know Him.

He opened the suture of the skull, entered through the gate which is called the Gate of Joy. He found three places in the body where He could live, three conditions where He could move; waking, dreaming, sleeping.

He entered the body, named its various parts, wondered if there could be anything there not Himself, rejoiced to find there was nothing but Himself.

Hence He is known by the name Idandra—He that sees—or it is shortened into Indra; for even the gods are affectionate.

5

First He becomes the seed of a man, which is light gathered from all the limbs of the body. Man nourishes himself within himself as seed. When he ejects that seed into a woman, he himself is born. That is his first incarnation.

The seed merges in the woman's body; because it becomes her body, it does not harm her. She nourishes the self of the man within herself.

Protect her, for she is protecting the seed. Before and after the birth of the child, man blesses the child, blessing himself. Man lives in his child; that is his second incarnation.

The son being the father over again, carries the traditions of the family, and the father having completed his fate, exhausted his years, dies and is born again. That is his third incarnation.

Sage Wamadewa said: "When lying in the womb, I understood how the gods worked. They put me into that iron-gated, hundred-gated, prison but I fled quickly, fled like a hawk.'

Sage Wamadewa, broke out of the body, did all that he desired, attained the Kingdom of Heaven, became immortal; yes, became immortal.

"On whom should we meditate as the Self? Which of the two is He? Is He that by which we see, hear, speak, smell, separate the sweet from the sour?

Or is He that other, living in the mind or in the intellect as imagination, discrimination, knowledge, continuity, intuition, conviction, contemplation, will, emotion, memory, desire, resolution, being, living, loving, longing; all names for the one Intelligence?

He is Spirit, Creator, God; all gods; earth, air, water, wind, fire, constituents of life, all greater and lesser combinations; seminal, egg-born, womb-born, sweat-born, soil-born; horses, cows, men, elephants, birds; everything that breathes, movable, immovable: all founded upon, all moved by the one Intelligence. Intelligence is Spirit.

Sage Wamadewa, with this knowledge, did all that he desired, left this world for Heaven, became immortal; became immortal.

XI

The Doctrine of the Chandogyas
Chandogya Upanishad

Book VI

1

Speech, eyes, ears, limbs, life, energy, come to my help. These books have Spirit for theme. I shall never deny Spirit, nor Spirit deny me. Let me be in union, communion with Spirit. When I am one with Spirit, may the laws these books proclaim live in me, may the laws live.

2

Once upon a time there lived Shwetaketu, son of Uddalaka. Uddalaka said: "My son! Find a teacher, learn; none of our family has remained a Brahman in name only."

At twelve he found his teacher; at twenty-four, having completed the study of the Wedas, he returned home, stiff-necked, arrogant, self-willed.

Uddalaka said: "My son! You think such a lot of yourself, but did you ask your teacher about that initiation, which makes a man hear what is not heard, think what is not thought, know what is not known?"

"What is that initiation, Lord?" said Shwetaketu. Uddalaka said: "By knowing a lump of clay you know all things made of clay;

they differ from one another as it were in language and in name, having no reality but their clay;

By knowing one nugget of gold you know all things made of gold; they differ from one another as it were in language and in name, having no reality but their gold;

By knowing one piece of base metal you know all things made of that metal; they differ from one another as it were in language and in name, having no reality but that metal.

For the like reason, after that initiation, you know everything."

Shwetaketu said: "My revered teacher cannot have known that; had he known it he would have told me. Therefore, Lord! teach it."

Uddalaka said: "I will teach it, my son!"

3

"My son! In the beginning, there was mere being, one without a second. Some say there was mere nothing, nothing whatsoever; that everything has come out of nothing.

But how can that be true, my son, said Uddalaka; how could that which is, come from that which is not?

I put it otherwise; in the beginning there was mere being, one without a second.

That being thought: 'Would that I were many! I will create.' He created light. Light thought: 'Would that I were many! I will create!' Light created the waters. When anybody weeps or sweats, the tears and the sweat are created by light.

Those waters thought: 'Would that we were many! We will create!' They created food. Whenever and wherever it rains, food is abundant. Food is from water.'

4

There are three classes of creatures: the egg-born, the womb-born, the soil-born.

That divine Being thought: 'I will go into the three gods—light, water, food. I will give them not only life, but names and shapes.'

He said: 'I will make each of them threefold.' He and life went into the three gods, and He gave them names and shapes.

You shall hear, my son, how He divides each of the three gods into three, and each of these three into three again.'

5

Whatever redness is in fire is a shape of light; whatever whiteness, a shape of water; whatever blackness, a shape of food. So fire as fire disappears, its shape is a name or way of talking; reality lies in the first three gods.

Whatever redness is in sun is a shape of light; whatever whiteness a shape of water} whatever blackness a shape of food. So sun as sun disappears, its shape is a name or way of talking; reality lies in the first three gods.

Whatever redness is in moon is a shape of light; whatever whiteness a shape of water; whatever blackness a shape of food. So moon as moon disappears, its shape is a name or way of talking; reality lies in the first three gods.

Whatever redness is in lightning is a shape of light; whatever whiteness a shape of water; whatever blackness a shape of food. So lightning as lightning disappears, its shape is a name or way of talking; reality lies in the first three gods.

The great householders of the past, men famous for their learning and wisdom, had this in mind when they said: 'Let no man say there is anything we have not heard, thought, seen.' They knew everything.

They knew that redness, no matter where found, was always light, whiteness always water, blackness always food.

They knew that a thing, no matter how strange it looked, was but some combination of those three first gods.

My son, when the three gods enter into man, each of those three divides into three.

6

Food when drunk is changed into three qualities— the grossest becomes excrement; the finest mind; whatever is midway, flesh.

Water when drunk is changed into three qualities— the grossest becomes urine; the finest becomes life; whatever is midway, blood.

Light when we eat it in fat or oil, is changed into three qualities—the grossest becomes bone; the finest speech; whatever is midway, marrow.

Remember, my son! mind comes from food, life comes from water, speech comes from light."

"Explain once more, Lord!" said Shwetaketu.

"I will explain, my son!" said Uddalaka.

7

"The finest quality of curds, when churned, rises up as butter.

So the finest quality of the food we swallow, rises up as mind.

The finest quality of the water we swallow, rises up as life.

The finest quality of the light we swallow, rises up as speech.

Remember, my son! mind comes from food, life comes from water, speech comes from light."

"Explain once more, Lord!" said Shwetaketu.

"I will explain, my son!" said Uddalaka.

8

"Man has sixteen phases. Abstain from food for a fortnight if you will, but drink j if you cut off drink, you cut off life."

Shwetaketu having abstained from food for a fortnight, went to his father and said: "What is the lesson today?"

Uddalaka asked him to repeat Rig-Weda, Yajur-Weda, Sama-Weda verses.

Shwetaketu said: "I do not remember them."

Uddalaka said: "A coal no bigger than a fire-fly would not make a blaze bigger than itself, so, my son, since only one of your sixteen phases remains, you cannot remember the Wedas. Now go and eat; then you will understand me."

Shwetaketu having taken food, went to his father again, answered all his questions.

Uddalaka said: "My son! A coal no bigger than a firefly if fed with hay makes a blaze bigger than itself. One phase that remained out of sixteen fed with food blazed up, and now you can remember the Wedas.

Remember, my son! mind comes from food, life comes from water, speech comes from light."

Shwetaketu understood what he said; understood what his father said.

9

Aruna's son, Uddalaka said to Shwetaketu: "My son! know the nature of sleep. When a man sleeps, he is united with that Being, that is himself. We think it enough to say that he sleeps, yet he sleeps with himself.

A tethered bird, after flying in every direction, settles down on its perch; the mind, after wandering in every direction, settles down on its life; for, my son! mind is tethered to life.

Know the nature of hunger and thirst. Man becomes hungry. Water brings his food to his belly. Water brings his food, as cowherd his cow, horseman his horse, general his army. Remember, my son! that body sprouts from food; could it sprout without a root?

What is the root of all? What but food?

Remember, my son! water is root, food its sprout; light is root, water its sprout; in the same way, that Being is root, light its sprout. All creatures have their root in that Being. He is their rock, their home.

Man becomes thirsty. Light brings the water to his gullet, as cowherd his cow, horseman his horse, general his army. Remember, my son! that food sprouts from water; could it sprout without a root?

What is the root of all? What but water?

Light is root, water its sprout; that Being is root, light its sprout. All creatures have their root in that Being; He is their rock, their home. My son! I have already told you how the three first gods became each of them threefold when in contact with body. When a man is dying, his speech merges into mind, his mind into life, his life into light, his light into the one Being.

That Being is the seed; all else but His expression. He is truth, He is Self. Shwetaketu! You are That."

"Explain once more, Lord!" said Shwetaketu.

"I will explain!" said Uddalaka.

10

"My son! Bees create honey by gathering the sweet juices from different flowers, and mixing all into a common juice.

And there is nothing in honey whereby the juice of a particular flower can be identified, so it is with the various creatures who merge in that Being, in deep sleep or in death.

Whatever they may be, tiger, lion, wolf, bear, worm, moth, gnat, mosquito, they become aware of particular life when they are born into it or awake.

That Being is the seedj all else but His expression. He is truth. He is Self. Shwetaketu! You are That."

"Explain once more, Lord!" said Shwetaketu.

"I will explain!" said Uddalaka.

11

"My son! Rivers, flowing east and west, rise from the sea, return to the sea, become the sea itself, forget their identities.

These creatures do not know that they have risen from that Being, or returned to that Being.

Whatever that may be, tiger, lion, wolf, boar, worm, moth, gnat, mosquito, they become aware of particular life when they are born into it or awake.

That Being is the seed; all else but His expression. He is truth. He is Self. Shwetaketu! You are That."

"Explain once more, Lord!" said Shwetaketu.

"I will explain!" said Uddalaka.

12

"Strike at the bole of a tree, sap oozes but the tree lives; strike at the middle of the tree, sap oozes but the tree lives; strike at the top of the tree, sap oozes but the tree lives. The Self as life, fills the tree; it flourishes in happiness, gathering its food through its roots.

If life leaves one branch, that branch withers. If life leaves a second branch, that branch withers. If life leaves a third branch, that branch withers. When life leaves the whole tree, the whole tree withers.

Remember, my son! The body bereft of Self dies. Self does not die.

That Being is the seed; all else but His expression. He is truth. He is Self. Shwetaketu! You are That."

"Explain once more, Lord!" said Shwetaketu.

"I will explain!" said Uddalaka.

13

Uddalaka asked his son to fetch a banyan fruit. "Here it is, Lord!" said Shwetaketu. "Break it'" said Uddalaka. "I have broken it, Lord!" "What do you see there?" "Little seeds, Lord!" "Break one of them, my son!" "It is broken, Lord!" "What do you see there?" "Nothing, Lord!" said Shwetaketu. Uddalaka said: "My son! This great banyan tree has sprung up from seed so small that you cannot see it. Believe in what I say, my son!

That Being is the seed; all else but His expression. He is truth. He is Self. Shwetaketu! You are That."

"Explain once more, Lord!" said Shwetaketu.

"I will explain!" said Uddalaka.

14

"Put this salt into water, see me tomorrow morning," said Uddalaka. Shwetaketu did as he was told.

Uddalaka said: "Bring me the salt you put into water last night."

Shwetaketu looked, but could not find it. The salt had dissolved.

Uddalaka asked his son how the top of the water tasted. Shwetaketu said: "It is salt."

Uddalaka asked how the middle of the water tasted.

Shwetaketu said: "It is salt."

Uddalaka asked how the bottom of the water tasted.

Shwetaketu said: "It is salt."

Uddalaka said: "Throw away the water; come to me."

Shwetaketu did as he was told and said: "The salt will always remain in the water."

Uddalaka said: "My son! Though you do not find that Being in the world, He is there.

That Being is the seed; all else but His expression. He is truth. He is Self. Shwetaketu! You are That."

"Explain once more, Lord!" said Shwetaketu.

"I will explain!" said Uddalaka.

15

"My son! If a man were taken out of the province of Gandhara, abandoned in a forest blindfolded, he would turn here and there, he would shout: 'I have been brought here blindfolded and abandoned!'

Thereupon some good man might take off the bandage and say: 'Go in that direction; Gandhara is there.' The bandage off, he would, if a sensible man, ask his way from village to village and come at last to Gandhara. In the same way the man initiated by his master, finds his way back into himself. Having remained in his body till all his Karma is spent, he is joined to Himself.

That Being is the seed; all else but His expression. He is truth. He is Self. Shwetaketu! You are That."

"Explain once more, Lord!" said Shwetaketu.

"I will explain!" said Uddalaka.

16

"Relations gather round a sick man and say: 'Do you remember me? Do you remember me?' He remembers until his speech has merged in his mind, his mind in his life, his life in his light, his light in the one Being.

When his speech is merged in his mind, his mind in his life, his life in his light, his light in that one Being, what can he remember?

That Being is the seed; all else but His expression. He is truth. He is Self. Shwetaketu! You are That."

"Explain once more, Lord!" said Shwetaketu.

"I will explain!" said Uddalaka.

17

"My son! They bring a man in handcuffs to the magistrate, charging him with theft. The magistrate orders the hatchet to be heated. If the man has committed the theft and denies it, he is false to himself, and having nothing but that lie to protect him, grasps the hatchet; and is burned,

If he has not committed the theft, he is true to himself and, with truth for his protector, grasps the hatchet; and is not burned. He is acquitted.

The man that was not burnt, lived in truth. Remember that all visible things live in truth; remember that truth and Self are one. Shwetaketu! You are That."

Shwetaketu understood what he said, yes, he understood what his father said.

Book VII

1

Narada asked Sage Sanatkumar to teach him.

Sanatkumar said: "Say what you know; I will say what you do not."

Narada said: "Lord! I know Rig-Weda, Yajur-Weda, Sama-Weda, Atharwa-Weda, histoiy and tradition called the fifth Weda, grammar, ritual, mathematics, astrology, mineralogy, logic, economics, physics, metaphysics, zoology, politics, astronomy, mechanics, fine arts.

Lord! Yet these things are but elementary knowledge; I do not know the Self. I have heard from masters, that he who knows Self, goes beyond sorrow. I am lost in sorrow. Help me to go beyond."

Sanatkumar said: "All your knowledge is but the knowledge of names. The four Wedas, grammar, ritual and the like, all that is but a name. Worship name as Spirit.

Who worships name as Spirit, moves within the limits of what is named, as it may please him, provided he worships it as nothing but Spirit."

"Is there anything above name?" said Narada.

"Yes," said Sanatkumar.

"Explain it, Lord!" said Narada.

2

Sanatkumar said: "Speech is above name. Through speech we understand not only the Wedas, grammar, ritual and the like but heaven, earth, wind, air, Water, fire, men, gods, cattle, birds, herbs, trees, beasts, worms, midges, ants, right, wrong, true, false, good, evil, pleasant, unpleasant. Without speech who could explain right, wrong; good, evil; pleasant, unpleasant? Speech explains all. Worship speech.

Who worships speech as Spirit, moves within the limits of what is spoken, as it may please him, provided he worships it as nothing but Spirit."

"Is there anything above speech?" said Narada.

3

"Yes," said Sanatkumar. "Mind is above speech. A closed fist holds two acorns, two berries, two nuts; so mind holds both speech and name.

When man thinks of reading Wedas, he reads them; when he thinks of doing, he does; when he thinks of children and cattle, he wants them; when he thinks of this world or the next, he wants it. Mind is Self. Mind is world. Mind is Spirit, Worship mind.

Who worships mind as Spirit, moves within the limits of what is thought, as it may please him, provided he worships mind as nothing but Spirit."

"Is there anything above mind?" said Narada.

4

"Yes," said Sanatkumar. "Will is above mind. When man wills he thinks, calls up speech which breaks into names. Sentences are made out of words, actions are made out of thoughts.

Everything is founded on will; everything forms will; everything lives in will. Heaven and earth will; wind and air will; water and light will; rain wills because water and light will; food wills because rain wills; life wills because food wills; speech wills because life wills; actions will because speech wills; world wills because actions will; everything wills because world wills. Such is will. Worship will.

Who worships will as Spirit, obtains the world he wills, attains the eternal by his will for the eternal, attains honor by his will for honor, attains the sorrow-less by his will to go beyond sorrow. Who worships will as Spirit, moves within the limits of what is willed, as it may please him, provided he worships will as nothing but Spirit."

"Is there anything above will?" said Narada.

5

"Yes," said Sanatkumar. "Mind's mother substance is above will.

When that is stirred, man wills; thinks, calls up speech; which breaks forth in words. Sentences are made of names; actions are made of thoughts.

Yes, these are founded on mind's mother substance. They form that substance, they live in substance. Man may be learned in names, but if that substance is absent, he is absent; he is ignored by everybody, the names go for nothing. Everybody listens to a man, no matter how light his learning, if substance be there. Therefore that substance is the abode of all. That substance is Self, is rock. Worship the mind's mother substance.

Who worships that as Spirit, moves within the limits of all that it contains, as it may please him, provided he worships it as nothing but Spirit. He attains the eternal by becoming eternal, he attains the unchanging by becoming unchanging, attains joy, becomes joy."

"Is there anything above that substance?" said Narada.

6

"Yes," said Sanatkumar. "Meditation is above substance. Earth, sky, heaven, water, mountain, men, gods, meditate. The greatness of the great comes from meditation. Small men quarrel, deceive, denounce; great men meditate, enjoy the greatness that it brings. Worship meditation.

Who worships meditation as Spirit, moves within the limits of its subject, as it may please him, provided he worships meditation as nothing but Spirit."

"Is there anything above meditation?" said Narada.

7

"Yes," said Sanatkumar. "Wisdom is above meditation. Through wisdom we understand the four Wedas, history, tradition, grammar, ritual and all the other sciences; heaven, earth, wind, air, water, fire, men, gods, cattle, birds, herbs, trees, beasts, worms, midges, ants, right, wrong, true, false, good, evil, pleasant, unpleasant, food and its taste, this world and the next. Worship wisdom.

Who worships wisdom as Spirit, attains all knowledge and experience; moves within the limits of its subject, as it may please him, provided he worships wisdom as nothing but Spirit."

"Is there anything above wisdom?" said Narada.

8

"Yes," said Sanatkumar. "Power is above wisdom. One powerful man terrifies a hundred wise men. When man becomes powerful, he rises; as he rises, he serves} as he serves, he associates with the wise; in consultation with the wise,-he sees, hears, thinks, knows, acts; becomes wise. Through power we are masters of earth, sky, heaven, mountain, men, gods, cattle, herbs, trees, beasts, worms, midges and ants. Worship power.

Who worships power as Spirit, moves within the limits of the powerful, as it may please him, provided he worships power as nothing but Spirit."

"Is there anything above power?" said Narada.

9

"Yes," said Sanatkumar. "Food is above power. If a man abstain from food for even ten days, though he may live, he cannot see, hear, think, discriminate, act or know. When he eats, he will see, hear, think, discriminate, act and know. Worship food.

Who worships food as Spirit, he obtains food and drink as much as he likes, moves within the limits of all that eat, as it may please him, provided he worships food as nothing but Spirit."

"Is there anything above food?" said Narada.

10

"Yes," said Sanatkumar. "Water is above food. When rain fails creatures fall sick for lack of food; when there is enough rain there is enough food, and they rejoice. All are images made of water; earth, sky, heaven, mountain, men, gods, cattle, herbs, trees, beasts, down to worms, midges, ants. Worship water.

Who worships water as Spirit gets everything he wants, becomes contented, moves within the limits of all that drink, as it may please him, provided he worships water as nothing but Spirit."

"Is there anything above water?" said Narada.

11

"Yes," said Sanatkumar. "Light is above water. When light quiets wind, heats air, people say: 'It burns, it boils, it will rain.' First, light; then water. Light makes thunder roll, light makes lightning strike, whether above or below. People say: 'There is thunder, it will rain.' Light first; then water. Worship light.

Who meditates on light as Spirit, becomes bright, attains the receptacles of light, full of brilliance without darkness; moves within the limits of all that is bright, as it may please him, provided he worships light as nothing but Spirit."

"Is there anything above light?" said Narada.

12

"Yes," said Sanatkumar. "Air is above light. Sun, moon, lightning, star, fire, live in air; through air we speak, through air we hear, through air the echo comes. Man enjoys through air, he is born in air, grows in air, enjoys in air. Worship air.

Who worships air as Spirit, attains the receptacles of light, free from sorrow, free from bondage; moves within the limits of air, as it may please him, provided he worships air as nothing but Spirit."

"Is there anything above air?" said Narada.

13

"Yes," said Sanatkumar. "Memory is above air. Take away memory from men, they no longer hear, think, or understand. Give back their memory, they hear, think and understand. Through memory we recognise our children and our cattle. Worship memory.

Who worships memory as Spirit, moves within the limits of his memory, as it may please him, provided he worships memory as nothing but Spirit."

"Is there anything above memory?" said Narada.

14

"Yes," said Sanatkumar. "Hope is above memory. Fired with hope, man repeats the sacred words, does this or that, desires children and property, longs for life here and hereafter. Worship hope.

Who worships hope as Spirit, gets all he wants, never gives a blessing in vain, moves within the limits of his hope, as it may please him, provided he worships hope as nothing but Spirit."

"Is there anything above hope?" said Narada.

15

"Yes," said Sanatkumar. "Life is above hope. Spokes of a wheel are centered in the hub, everything is fixed in life. Life lives by life; life gives life; life gives for life. Life gives power. Life is father, mother, sister, brother, tutor and guide.

If a man speak cruel words to a father, mother, sister, brother, tutor or guide, people say: 'Shame upon you for such cruelty!' but if, life once gone, somebody shoves them back on to the funeral pyre with a poker, where is the cruelty?

Life is all. If a man feels and knows this, his reason is deeper than discussion. Should people say that his reason is deeper than discussion, he should not deny it. He who knows truth goes beyond discussion."

"Lord! I discuss and at length, that I may find truth," said Narada.

"What should we know but truth?" said Sanatkumar.

"Lord! I would know," said Narada.

16

"How can a man speak the truth, without knowing it. Man speaks what he knows. Then know."

"I would know, Lord!" said Narada.

17

"Thinking, man knows; unthinking, he cannot know. Therefore think."

"I would think, Lord!" said Narada.

18

"With faith, man thinks; faithless, he cannot think. Therefore have faith."

"I would have faith, Lord!" said Narada.

19

"From devotion, man gets faith; without devotion, he has none. Have devotion."

"I would have devotion, Lord!" said Narada.

20

"When man acts, he gets devotion; without action, he has none. Act."

"I would act, Lord!" said Narada.

21

"Man acts when he gets happiness; without happiness, he does nothing. Find happiness."

"I would be happy, Lord!" said Narada.

22

"Man gets happiness from the unlimited; from the limited, none. Find the unlimited."

"I would find the unlimited, Lord!" said Narada.

23

"Where man finds a thing, sees nothing else, hears nothing else, knows nothing else, that is the unlimited; where he finds a thing, sees something else, hears something else, knows something else, that is the limited. The unlimited is immortal; the limited is mortal."

"Lord! On what does the unlimited depend?" said Narada.

"On His own greatness," said Sanatkumar, "or not even that. The possession of cattle, horses, elephants; farms, mansions, servants, women, gold are greatness in this world. I do not call it greatness when one thing depends upon another. The unlimited depends on nothing."

24

"He is below, above, behind, in front, on the right, on the left; He is everything. If I put I instead of He, I say, I am below, I am above, I am behind, I am in front, I am on the right, I am on the left. I am everything.

I put Self instead of He, I say, the Self is below, above, behind, in front, to the right, to the left. The Self is everything. The personal Self is the impersonal Self.

He who sees, thinks, knows this, loves the Self, plays with the Self, unites with the Self, enjoys the Self, governs himself, moves himself everywhere at his pleasure. Those who think otherwise are governed by others. They lose what they gain. Nowhere can they move at their pleasure.

25

He who thinks, feels, knows this, draws life from himself, hope from himself, memory from himself ; air, light, water from himself; birth, death, food, power, knowledge, meditation, mind, will, speech, name, words, action, everything from himself.

He who knows this, cares nothing for death, cares nothing for disease, cares nothing for misery; looks at everything with the eye of Self; gets everything everywhere; remains one, though multiplied threefold, fivefold, sevenfold, eleven-fold, hundred-fold, hundred-and-eleven-fold, twenty-thousand-fold.'

Pure food creates pure intellect; pure intellect creates strong memory; strong memory cuts all the knots of the heart."

Sage Sanatkumar leads beyond the darkness those that have washed their impurities away. Hence men call him the Great

Commander, men call him the Great Commander.

Book VIII

1

In this body, in this town of Spirit, there is a little house shaped like a lotus, and in that house there is a little space. One should know what is there.

What is there? Why is it so important?

There is as much in that little space within the heart, as there is in the whole world outside. Heaven, earth, fire, wind, sun, moon, lightning, stars; whatever is and whatever is not, everything is there.

If everything is in man's body, every being, every desire, what remains when old age comes, when decay begins, when the body falls?

What lies in that space, does not decay when the body decays, nor does it fall when the body falls. That space is the home of Spirit. Every desire is there. Self is there, beyond decay and death; sin and sorrow; hunger and thirst ; His aim truth, His will truth. Man can live in the body as long as he obeys the law, as a man may live in a certain farm, in a certain town, in a certain province, or wherever he fancy, if he obey the law.

Earthly pleasures exhaust themselves ; heavenly pleasures exhaust themselves. Wherever men go without attaining Self or knowing truth, they cannot move at their pleasure; but after attaining Self and knowing truth, wherever they go, they move at their pleasure.

2

If man wants the company of his fathers, all he need do is to will it; they will appear and make him happy.

If he wants the company of his mothers, all he need do is to will it; they will appear and make him happy.

If he wants the company of his brothers, all he need do is to will it; they will appear and make him happy.

If he wants the company of his sisters, all he need do is to will it; they will appear and make him happy.

If he wants the company of his friends, all he need do is to will it; they will appear and make him happy.

If he wants women, all he need do is to will it; they will appear and make him happy.

If he wants perfume or flower, all he need do is to will it; it will appear and make him happy.

If he wants food or drink, all he need do is to will it; it will appear and make him happy.

If he wants a thing or a place, all he need do is to will it; it will appear and make him happy.

3

These wants are justified, but they are smothered by self-interest; it's because they are so smothered that an ignorant man cannot see the dead.

A wise man sees in Self, those that are alive, those that are dead; and gets what this world cannot give. An ignorant man treads on the ground, but does not know the gold that lies underneath ; we pass into the Self during sleep, but do not know Him.

Self stays in the heart; 'heart', a word that seems to say 'here it is'. Who knows this, daily enjoys the Kingdom of Heaven.

A wise man, leaving his body, joins that flame; is one with His own nature. That nature is Self, fearless immortal Spirit.

Whatever binds mortal and immortal, they call truth. Who knows this, daily enjoys the Kingdom of Heaven.

4

Self is the wall which keeps the creatures from breaking in. Day and night do not go near Him, nor age, nor death, nor grief, nor good, nor evil. Sin turns away from Him; for Spirit knows no sin.

Self is the bridge. When man crosses that bridge, if blind, he shall see; if sick, he shall be well; if unhappy, he shall be happy. When he crosses that bridge, though it be night, it shall be day; for heaven is shining always.

Heaven is for those that are masters of themselves. They can move anywhere in this world at their pleasure.

5

Sacrifice is to be master of one-self; for through that mastery a wise man knows the Self. Duty is to be master of one-self. Through mastery a wise man knows the Self.

Vows are the mastery of one-self; for through that mastery man gets the protection of the Self. Silence is the mastery of one-self for through that mastery man attains the meditation upon the Self.

Fasting is the mastery of one-self ; for through that mastery man shares the imperishability of the Self. A hermit's life is that mastery.

In the Kingdom of Heaven are the springs of doing and knowing that rise from Spirit itself; beyond spreads the lake of joy; beyond that blossoms the tree of immortality; beyond that lies the town of spirit, full of light built by the Lord.

But heaven is for those that find the springs of doing and knowings they can move anywhere in this world at their pleasure.

6

Orange, blue, yellow, red, are not less in man's arteries than in the sun.

As a long highway passes between two villages, one at either end, so the sun's rays pass between this world and the world beyond. They flow from the sun, enter into the arteries, flow back from the arteries, enter into the sun.

When man is asleep, enjoying his sleep, he creates no dream; his soul sleeps in the arteries. No evil can touch him, for he is filled with light.

When he is dying, those around him ask if he knows them; as long as the soul does not leave the body he knows them.

But when the soul leaves the body, ascending with the sun's rays, he meditates on Om and, with the speed of thought, goes to the sun. Sun is the Gate of Heaven, where the wise can pass.

Here is my authority: "There are a hundred and one arteries lead-ing to the heart; one of them pierces the crown of the head. He who goes upwards through it, attains immortality; He who does not, is born again."

7

Prajapati said: "Self is free from sin and sorrow; decay and death; hunger and thirst. His aim is truth; His will is truth. Find Him; know Him. Who finds and knows Him, gets what he wants, goes where he likes."

The godly and the godless both came to know what Prajapati said and thought: We swear by our souls, we must find that Self, by which we shall get whatever we want, go wherever we like.

Indra from among the godly, Wirochana from among the godless, went to Prajapati, with folded hands, without letting one another know.

They stayed with him for thirty-two days, observing the vows; when Prajapati asked for what they stayed, they said: "Everyone knows that you have said that Self is free from sin and sorrow; decay and death; hunger and thirst. His aim is truth; His will is truth. Find Him; know Him. Who finds and knows Him, gets what he wants, goes where he likes. We hope to attain that Self, and therefore stay."

Prajapati said: "That Person seen in the eye is Self. That is unalarmed, immortal Spirit."

They said: "Lord! Which of the two is Self, the one reflected in water, or the one reflected in a mirror?"

Prajapati said: "He is reflected in both, reflected everywhere."

Prajapati said: "Look at yourself in a bowl of water; come again if you do not understand the Self."

They looked into the bowl of water.

Prajapati said: "What did you see there?"

They said: "We saw ourselves; our doubles; even with our hair and nails."

Prajapati said: "Shave, put on fine clothes, fine jewels; look into the water again."

They did accordingly.

Prajapati said: "What did you see?"

They said: "Lord! We saw ourselves shaven, dressed, adorned."

Prajapati said: "That is Self. That is unalarmed, immortal Spirit."

They both went away satisfied.

Prajapati said to himself: "They go without finding the Self, without knowing the Self. Who follows their philosophy, whether godly or godless, perishes."

Wirochana, perfectly satisfied, went to the godless and preached to them his philosophy: "Body alone is important; body alone is to be adored. Who knows the importance of body and adores it, gets everything in this world and the next."

Hence even today a man who has no faith, no devotion, no charity, is called godless; for that is the philosophy of the godless. They supply the dead with food, clothes, jewelry; they think thereby to attain heaven.

9

But Indra, before he returned to the godly, saw the snare. He thought to himself: "If the body is adorned, so is its reflection; if it is well dressed, so is its reflection; if it is clean, so is its reflection; but then if the body were blind, Self would be blind; if the body were lame, Self would be lame; if the body were crippled, Self would be crippled; if the body were dead, Self would be dead. I see no good in this."

He went back with folded hands.

Prajapati said: "Indra! you went away with Wirochana, perfectly satisfied. What brings you back?"

Indra said: "Lord! If the body is shaven, dressed, adorned, so is its reflection; but if the body were blind, lame, crippled, Self would be blind, lame, crippled; if the body were dead, Self would be dead. I see no good in this."

Prajapati said: "Indra! This bodily Self is like that. Stay for another thirty-two days; I will explain more."

Indra stayed accordingly; Prajapati said:

10

"The Self is the Adorable, who moves in dreams. He is the unalarmed, immortal Spirit."

Indra went away satisfied but, before he reached the godly, saw the snare. He thought within himself: 'Self that dreams is not blind, if body is blind; Self is not lame, if body is lame; Self is not affected by the defects of body.

He is not killed when body is killed; he is not crippled when body is crippled; yet he is killed and chased in dreams; he is unhappy; now and again he weeps. I see no good in this.'

He went back with folded hands.

Prajapati said: "Indra! You went away satisfied. What brings you back?"

Indra said: "Lord! Self is not blind, because body is blind; Self is not crippled, because body is crippled; Self is not affected by the defects of body.

Self is not killed when body is killed. He is not lame, if body is lame. Self is killed and chased in dreams; He is unhappy; now and again He weeps. I see no good in this."

Prajapati said: "You are right. Stay for another thirty-two days; I will explain more."

Indra stayed accordingly; Prajapati said:

11

"When man is fast asleep, at peace with himself, happy, without a dream, then that is Self. That is the unalarmed, immortal Spirit."

Indra went away satisfied but, before he reached the godly, saw the snare. He thought within himself: 'Man in his sleep does not know that he is Self; neither does he know any other creatures. He is lost. I do not see any good in this.'

He went back with folded hands.

Prajapati asked: "Indra, you went away satisfied. What brings you back?"

Indra said: "Lord! Sleeping without a dream man does not know that he is Self, neither does he know any creatures. He is lost. I see no good in this."

Prajapati said: "Indra! You are right; yet where else can you find the Self? Stay for five days more; I will explain more."

Indra stayed accordingly. He stayed there for a hundred and one days in all; everybody knows that Indra stayed with Prajapati for a hundred and one days, mastering Self. Prajapati said to him:

12

"Indra! This mortal body is under sentence of death; nevertheless it is the house of the immortal; the un-embodied. So long as He is in body, He likes and He dislikes; so long as He is in body there is no escape. When He is without body, likes and dislikes do not touch Him.

Wind has no body; cloud, lightning, thunder have no body; but when they conjoin with light and rise in air, they show in their own shapes. Likewise that blessed Self, conjoint with light, rises from body, shows himself in His own shape. He moves in this world enjoying women, riding in conveyances, entertaining his friends, heedless of his body; as a master workman engages an assistant, Self engages life to look after his body.

Who sees through the eye, knowing that He sees, is Self, the eye an instrument whereby He sees; who smells through the nose, knowing that He smells, is Self, the nose an instrument whereby He smells; who speaks through the tongue, knowing that He speaks, is Self, the tongue an instrument whereby He speaks; who hears through the ear, knowing that He hears, is Self, the ear an instrument whereby He hears; who thinks through the mind, knowing that He thinks, is Self, the mind an instrument whereby

He thinks. He looks through the mind's eye, his spiritual eye; in that eye heaven is made and all desires arise; all these his joy.

Gods adore that Self; thereby go where they will; satisfy every desire. Who discovers and knows the Self, goes where he will; satisfies every desire.

13

I have been drifting from darkness to passion, from passion to darkness. Shaking off evil, as a horse shakes off his' loose hair, freeing myself from evil as the moon breaks free from the eclipse, attaining the aim of my life, I enter the Kingdom of Heaven, where there is nothing more to attain; I enter the Kingdom of Heaven.

14

Names and shapes but hang in air; in very truth they live in immortal Spirit. He is Self.

Grant that I may enter the audience chamber. Grant that I may become glory itself; the glory of saints, the glory of kings, the glory of merchants; grant that I attain the glory of all glories. Grant that I may never be bopn again."

15

The Creator gave this knowledge to Prajapati; Prajapati to Manu; Manu to mankind.

He who studies the Wedas rightly, under the right teacher, does the right by that teacher; returns home; settles himself as an householder in a sacred place, keeps his study of the Wedas, leads a holy life, turns his senses towards the Self, never asks anything of anyone unless upon pilgrimage, and leads such a life to the last, he attains the Kingdom of Heaven; he never returns.

X

Famous Debates In The Forest
Brihadaranyaka Upanishad

Book I

Lead me from the unreal to the real!

Lead me from darkness to light!

Lead me from death to immortality!

In the beginning all things were Self, in the shape of personality. He looked round, saw nothing but Himself. The first thing he said was, 'It is I.' Hence 'I' became His name. Therefore even now if you ask a man who he is, he first says, 'It is I, and gives what other name he has. He is the eldest of all. Because he destroyed all evil, he is called the first Person. He who knows this, destroys all evil, takes the first rank.

He became afraid; loneliness creates fear. He thought: 'As there is nothing but myself, why should I be afraid?' Then his fear passed away; there was nothing to fear, fear comes when there is a second.

As a lonely man is unhappy, so he was unhappy. He wanted a companion. He was as big as man and wife together; He divided himself into two, husband and wife were born.

Yadnyawalkya said: 'Man is only half himself; his wife is the other half.'

They joined and mankind was born.

She thought: 'He shall not have me again; he has created me from himself; I will hide myself.'

She then became a cow, he became a bull; they joined and cattle were born. She became a mare, he a stallion; she became a she-ass, he an ass; they joined and the hoofed animals were born. She became a she-goat, he a goat; she became a ewe, he a ram; they joined and goats and sheep were born. Thus He created everything down to ants, male and female.

Then he put his hand into his mouth and there created fire as if he were churning butter. He knew that He was this creation; that He created it from Himself; that He was the cause. Who knows, finds creation joyful.

When they say: 'Sacrifice to this or that god,' they talk of separate gods; but all gods are created by Him, and He is all gods.

Whatever is liquid He created from His seed. Everything in this world is eater or eaten. The seed is food and fire is eater.

He created the gods; created mortal men, created the immortals. Hence this creation is a miracle. He who knows, finds this miracle joyful.

This world was everywhere the same till name and shape began; then one could say: 'He has such a name and such a shape.' Even today everything is made different by name and shape.

Self entered into everything, even the tips of fingernails. He is hidden like the razor in its case.

Though He lives in this world and maintains it, the ignorant cannot see Him.

When he is breathing, they name Him breath; when speaking, they name Him speech} when seeing, they name Him eye ; when hearing, they name Him ear ; when thinking, they name Him mind. He is not wholly there. All these names are the names of His actions.

He who worships Him as the one or the other is ignorant, is imperfect; though he attain completely one or the other perfection. Let him worship Him as Self, where all these become the whole.

This Self brings everything; for thereby everything is known. He is the footprint that brings a man to his goal. He who knows this attains name and fame.

This Self is nearer than all else; dearer than son, dearer than wealth, dearer than anything. If a man call anything dearer than Self, say that he will lose what is dear; of a certainty he will lose it; for Self is God. Therefore one should worship Self as Love. Who worships Self as Love, his love never shall perish.

It is said everything can be got through the knowledge of Spirit. What is that knowledge?

In the beginning there was Spirit. It knew itself as Spirit; from that knowledge everything sprang up. Whosoever among gods, sages and men, got that knowledge, became Spirit itself. Sage Wamadewa knew it and sang 'I was Manu; I was the sun.'

Even today he who knows that he is Spirit, becomes Spirit, becomes everything; neither gods nor men can prevent him, for he has become themselves.

Who thinks of himself as separate from Self, and worships some other than Self, he is ignorant; becomes a sacrificial animal for the gods.

As many beasts serve a man, man serves the gods; if one beast is taken away, man is sorry, and much more sorry if many are taken away? For a like reason gods dislike men who get this knowledge.

In the beginning all things were Spirit, one and sole; hence He lacked power. He created the good kings. Indra, Waruna, Soma, Rudra, Parjanya, Yama, Mrityu, Eeshana, are the kings among gods.

Hence the king is above all men. The priest occupies a lower seat at the coronation. The priest confers the crown upon the king, is the root of the king's power.

Therefore though the king attain supremacy at the end of his coronation he sits below the priest and acknowledges him as the root of his power. So whoever destroys the priest, destroys his root. He sins; he destroys the good.

He still lacked power; therefore He created the traders, that are arrayed in guilds like those troups of the gods; Wasus, Rudras, Adityas, Maruts and Wishwedewas.

He still lacked power; therefore He created the laborer who, like the god Pushan, feeds all. This earth is Pushan, for it feeds everything everywhere.

He still lacked power; therefore He created the good law. That law is the power of the king; there is nothing higher than law. Even a weak man rules the strong with the help of law; law and the king are the same. Law is truth. Who speaks the truth, speaks the law; who speaks the law, speaks the truth; they are the same.

Thus Spirit became the priest, the ruler, the trader, the laborer. Among the gods, Spirit appeared as fire; among men He appeared as priest; He became the king whose duty is to rule; the trader, whose duty is to trade; the laborer, whose duty is to serve. People wish for a place among the gods through fire, for a place among mankind through the priest; for Spirit appeared in these two forms.

If a man leaves this kingdom without knowing that he owns the kingdom of Self, that Self is of no service to him; it remains like the unread Wedas, or a deed not done. No, even if he does a great meritorious deed without knowing the Self, that deed will exhaust itself in the end. Worship the kingdom of Self. He who worships the kingdom of Self, does that which is never exhausted; whatever he wants, he gets from himself.

Hence this Self is the goal of all creatures. As long as man makes offerings and sacrifices, he pleases the gods; as long as he studies the Wedas, he pleases the wise; as long as he offers libations and desires children, he pleases the fathers; as long as he gives food and shelter, he pleases mankind; as long as he gives fodder and water the beasts are pleased; if birds and beasts down to the ants are fed in his house, they are pleased. But everybody wishes good to the man who has this knowledge; everybody is good to the man who is good to him.

In the beginning there was the Self, one and sole. He thought: 'Let me have a wife that I may have children; let me have wealth that I may do something in the world,' Thus far desire can go; even if man wants more, he cannot get it.

A lonely man thinks of a wife and children, of wealth and work; and so long as he does not get any of these, he thinks he is incomplete. Yet he is already complete; his mind is himself; speech his wife; life his offspring; eyes are his human wealth, for through eyes he gets it; ears his divine wealth, for through ears he gets it; body his work, for through body he works. This is the fivefold sacrifice; it applies to man, animal, everything. Who knows this, gets everything.

Book II

There lived Gargya, son of Balaka, learned yet proud. He went to Janaka, the king of Benares, and said: 'I will teach you about Spirit.'

Janaka said: 'People flock to me, my name on their lips, yet I give you a hundred cows for that promise.'

Gargya said: 'I worship as Spirit the God that is in the sun.'

Janaka said: 'No, no; that is no right way to talk of Spirit. He transcends all being. I worship Him as the crowned king of all. Who worships Him as such, transcends all being, becomes the crowned king of all.'

Gargya said: 'I worship as Spirit the God that is in the moon.'

Janaka said: 'No, no; that is no right way to talk of Spirit. I worship Him as the great king, the heavenly drinker, clad in purity. Who worships Him as the great King, milks heaven and drinks it day by day. His food is never exhausted.'

Gargya said: 'I worship as Spirit the God that is in lightning.'

Janaka said: 'No, no; that is no right way to talk of Spirit. I worship Him as light. Who worships Him as light becomes enlightened ; his children become enlightened,'

Gargya said: 'I worship as Spirit the God that is in the air.'

Janaka said: 'No, no; that is no right way to talk of Spirit. I worship Him as the still and the full. Who worships Him as the full is blessed with children and cattle. His family shall never be cut off.'

Gargya said: 'I worship as Spirit the God that is in wind.'

Janaka said: 'No, no; that is no right way to talk of Spirit. I worship Him as that impregnable, unconquerable army. Who worships Him as that army conquers his enemies.'

Gargya said: 'I worship as Spirit the God that is in fire,'

Janaka said: 'No, no; that is no right way to talk of Spirit. I worship Him as the tolerant; for fire warms the good and the bad. Who worships Him as the tolerant becomes tolerant; his children become tolerant.'

Gargya said: 'I worship as Spirit the God that is in water.'

Janaka said: 'No, no; that is no right way to talk of Spirit. I worship Him as a reflection. Who worships Him as a reflection gets what he wants; nothing runs against him; his children reflect him.'

Gargya said: 'I worship as Spirit the God that is the mirror.'

Janaka said: 'No, no; that is no right way to talk of Spirit. I worship Him as beauty. Who worships Him as beauty becomes beautiful; his children become beautiful; he is adored by everybody.'

Gargya said: 'I worship as Spirit the God that is in the echo.'

Janaka said: 'No, no; that is no right way to talk of Spirit. I worship Him as life coming out of life. Who worships Him as life is blessed with abounding life. He does not die until all is spent.'

Gargya said: 'I worship as Spirit the God that is in the four quarters.'

Janaka said: 'No, no; that is no right way to talk of Spirit. I worship Him as my double, who never forsakes me. Who worships Him as his double is surrounded by friends; his neighbours do not forsake him.'

Gargya said: 'I worship as Spirit the God that is in the shadow.'

Janaka said: .'No, no; that is no right way to talk of Spirit. I worship Him as death. Who worships Him as death gets long life; he does not die too soon,'

Gargya said: 'I worship as Spirit the God that is in the body.'

Janaka said: 'No, no; that is no right way to talk of Spirit. I worship Him as a man. Who worships Him as a man gets the body he wants, his children get the bodies they want.'

Gargya became silent.

Janaka said: 'Is that all?'

Gargya said: 'That is all.'

Janaka said: 'Spirit is not so quickly known.'

Gargya said: 'I come to you as a pupil.'

Janaka said: 'It is unusual for a preacher to come to a king, to learn about Spirit. However, I will make you understand Him clearly.'

He took him by the hand and rose. The two came to a sleeping man. Janaka called out: 'Mighty man! Pure man! Heavenly drinker!' He did not wake; he woke when Janaka took him by the hand.

Janaka said: 'Where was this man's knowing Self when he slept, whence came he when he woke?'

Gargya could not understand.

Janaka said: 'When he slept, the knowing Self, all the senses within it, lay at rest in the hollow of the heart. When Self has mastered sense, man is said to sleep.

Life is absorbed; speech, sight, hearing, thinking, absorbed.

'But when Self moves in dreams, He becomes his dreams. He becomes a great king; he becomes a great priest; he becomes the high and the low. As a great king surrounded by his retinue moves in his own country at his pleasure, Self, surrounded by his senses, moves in his own body, at his pleasure.

'But when man is in deep sleep he knows nothing; Self having crept out of those seventy-two thousand arteries called the Hita, which spread from the heart through all the body, goes to rest surrounded by his body. Whether a child, or a king or a holy man, he transcends all happiness and goes to sleep. Thus it is that Self goes to sleep.

'As threads come from the spider, as little sparks come from the fire, so all senses, all conditions, all gods, all beings, come from this Self. He is known as the "Truth of all truths". The senses are true, but He is the truth of them all.'

Book III

Spirit has two aspects: measurable, immeasurable; mortal, immortal; stable, unstable; graspable, ungraspable.

Everything on this earth except wind and sky is measurable, mortal, stable, graspable; it comes from the graspable, from the sun that shines in the heavens, the substance of the graspable.

Wind and sky are immeasurable, immortal, unstable, ungraspable; they come from the ungraspable, from God that shines through the sun, the substance of the ungraspable.

This is the material aspect of Spirit.

Now the divine aspect of Spirit.

Everything in the body except life and heart is measurable, mortal, stable, graspable; it comes from the graspable, from the eye, the substance of the graspable.

Life and heart are immeasurable, immortal, unstable, ungraspable; they come from the ungraspable, from God that shines in the right eye, the substance of the ungraspable.

And what is the shape of that God? It is like a saffron-colored garment, like a white woolen garment, like red cochineal, like the flame of fire, like the white lotus, like a sudden flash of lightning. Who knows Him thus, his glory flashes like lightning.

They describe Spirit as 'Not this; not that'. The first means: 'There is nothing except Spirit': the second means: There is nothing beyond Spirit.' They call Spirit the 'Truth of all truths'. The senses are true, but He is the truth of them all.

Book IV

Yadnyawalkya said to Maitreyee: 'Dear! I am going to renounce the world: I wish to divide my property between you and Katyayanee.'

Maitreyee said: 'Lord! If I get the wealth of the world, will it make me immortal?'

Yadnyawalkya said: 'No, your life will be like the life of the wealthy. There is no hope of immortality through wealth.'

Maitreyee said: 'What can I do with that which cannot make me immortal? Tell me what you know of immortality.'

Yadnyawalkya said: 'Well spoken! You were dear to me; those words have made you dearer. Come, sit down. I will explain; meditate on what I say.'

He continued: 'Of a certainty, the wife does not love her husband for himself but loves him for herself only.

> *The husband does not love his wife for herself, but loves her for himself only.*
>
> *The father does not love his sons for themselves, but loves them for himself only.*
>
> *A man does not love his wealth for itself, but loves it for himself only.*
>
> *A man does not love the priests for themselves, but loves them for himself only.*
>
> *A man does not love the rulers for themselves, but loves them for himself only.*
>
> *A man does not love the community for itself, but loves it for himself only.*
>
> *A man does- not love the gods for themselves, but loves them for himself only.*
>
> *A man does not love the creatures for themselves, but loves them for himself only.*
>
> *A man does not love anything for itself, but loves it for himself only.*

Maitreyee! This Self deserves to be seen, heard, thought of, meditated upon. When this Self is seen, heard, thought of, known, everything becomes known.

The priestly order ignores the man who thinks of it as anything apart from the Self.

The ruling order ignores the man who thinks of it as anything apart from the Self.

The community ignores the man who thinks of it as anything apart from the Self.

The gods ignore the man who thinks of them as anything apart from the Self.

The creatures ignore the man who thinks of them as anything apart from the Self.

Everything ignores the man who thinks of it as anything apart from the Self.

Hence this Self is the priest, the ruler; He is all gods, all men, all creatures, all that exists ; for these are

> *As the sounds of a drum that cannot be understood unless we understand the drum and the drummer;*
>
> *As the sounds of a conch that cannot be understood unless we understand the conch and the blower;*
>
> *As the sounds of a lute that cannot be understood unless we understand the lute and the player.*
>
> *As clouds of smoke come from fire kindled with damp fuel, from the great Being come the Rig-Weda, Yajur-Weda, Sama-Weda, Atharwa-Weda, history, ancient knowledge, sciences, Upanishads, poetry, aphorisms, commentaries, explanations. These are His breath.*
>
> *As all waters belong to the sea, all touches to the skin, all smells to the nose, all tastes to the tongue, all beauties to the eye, all words to the ear, all thoughts to the mind, all*

knowledge to the intellect, all works to the hand, all journeys to the feet, all Wedas to speech} so everything belongs to Him.

As a lump of salt thrown in water dissolves, and cannot be taken out again as salt, though wherever we taste the water it is salt, so this great endless deathless Being dissolved is knowledge; He reveals Himself with the elements, disappears when they disappear; leaving no name behind.

Maitreyee said: 'You say, Lord! that after death no name is left behind; this has confounded me,'

Yadnyawalkya said: 'Maitreyee! I say nothing that should confound you. It is easy to understand.

'For as long as there is duality, one sees the other, one smells the other, one hears the other, one speaks to the other, one thinks of the other, one knows the other; but when everything is one Self, who can see another, how can he see another; who can smell another, how can he smell another; who can hear another, how can he hear another ; who can speak to another, how can he speak to another; who can think of another, how can he think of another; who can know another, how can he know another? Maitreyee! How can the knower be known?'

Book V

This earth is the honey of all beings; all beings the honey of this earth. The bright eternal Self that is in earth, the bright eternal Self that lives in this body, are one and the same; that is immortality, that is Spirit, that is all.

Water is the honey of all beings; all beings the honey of water. The bright eternal Self that is in water, the bright eternal Self that lives in human seed, are one and the same; that is immortality, that is Spirit, that is all.

Fire is the honey of all beings; all beings the honey of fire. The bright eternal Self that is in fire, the bright eternal Self that lives in speech, are one and the same; that is immortality, that is Spirit, that is all.

Wind is the honey of all beings; all beings the honey of wind. The bright eternal Self that is in wind, the bright eternal Self that lives in breath, are one and the same; that is immortality, that is Spirit, that is all.

The sun is the honey of all beings; all beings the honey of the sun. The bright eternal Self that is in the sun, the bright eternal Self that lives in the eye, are one and the same; that is immortality, that is Spirit, that is all.

The quarters are the honey of all beings; all beings the honey of the quarters. The bright eternal Self that is in the quarters, the bright eternal Self that lives in the ear, are one and the same; that is immortality, that is Spirit, that is all.

The moon is the honey of all beings; all beings the honey of the moon. The bright eternal Self that is in the moon, the bright eternal Self that lives in the mind, are one and the same; that is immortality, that is Spirit, that is all.

Lightning is the honey of all beings, all beings the honey of lightning. The bright eternal Self that is in lightning, the bright eternal Self that lives in the light of the body, are one and the same; that is immortality, that is Spirit, that is all.

Thunder is the honey of all beings; all beings the honey of thunder. The bright eternal Self that is in thunder, the bright eternal Self that lives in the voice, are one and the same; that is immortality, that is Spirit, that is all.

Air is the honey of all beings; all beings the honey of air. The bright eternal Self that is in air, the bright eternal Self that lives in the hollow of the heart, are one and the same; that is immortality, that is Spirit, that is all.

Law is the honey of all beings; all beings are the honey of law. The bright eternal Self that is in law, the bright eternal Self that lives as the law in the body, are one and the-same; that is immortality, that is Spirit, that is all.

Truth is the honey of all beings; all beings the honey of truth. The bright eternal Self that is truth, the bright eternal Self that lives as the truth in man, are one and the same ; that is immortality, that is Spirit, that is all.

Mankind is the honey of all beings ; all beings the honey of mankind. The bright eternal Self that is in mankind, the bright eternal Self that lives in a man, are one and the same ; that is immortality, that is Spirit, that is all.

Self is the honey of all beings ; all beings the honey of Self. The bright eternal Self that is everywhere, the bright eternal Self that lives in a man, are one and the same; that is immortality, that is Spirit, that is all.

This Self is the Lord of all beings ; as all spokes are knit together in the hub, all things, all gods, all men, all lives, all bodies, are knit together in that Self.

This is the honey that Dadheechi gave to Ashwineekumars. A sage said to Ashwineekumars: 'As a reward for cutting off his head and substituting a horse's head Dadheechi gave you this honey, daring man! I proclaim this news, as thunder proclaims the rain. Dadheechi kept his word; though this honey was his secret, he gave it; gave this secret of creation.

'He made the two-footed; He made the four-footed. He, the great god, became the bird, entered into its body. He is the God who lives in all bodies. There is nothing that does not fill Him; nothing that He does not fill.

He wanted every form, for He wanted to show Himself; as a magician He appears in many forms, He masters hundreds and thousands of powers. He is those powers; those millions of powers, those innumerable powers. He is Spirit; without antecedent, without precedent, without inside, without outside; omnipresent, omniscient. Self is Spirit. That is revelation.'

Book VI

Adoration to the highest Self.

King Janaka of Behar sacrificed. Costly gifts were given to the priests. Many priests from the provinces of Kuru and Panchala had come. Janaka wanted to find out who knew most. He bought a thousand cows, every cow had ten gold coins tied between its horns.

He said: 'Venerable Priests! Let him, who knows Spirit, take those cows.'

But the priests dared not.

Thereupon Yadnyawalkya said to his pupil: 'Sama-shrawa! my son, take these cows.' He obeyed.

The other priests were angry. They said: 'How dare he call himself the wisest among us?'

Ashwala, a priest attached to the court of Janaka, said: 'Yadnyawalkya! Do you think you are the wisest among us?'

Yadnyawalkya said: 'I bow to him who knows Spirit. I wanted the cows.'

Ushasta, son of Chakra, said: 'Yadnyawalkya! Explain that Spirit, which out of sight is known by sight; that Self who lives in the hearts of all.'

Yadnyawalkya said: 'Your own Self lives in the hearts of all.'

Ushasta said: 'What Self do you say lives in the hearts of all?'

Yadnyawalkya said: 'He who inhales with the help of Prana is your Self, living in the hearts of all. He who exhales with the help of Apana is your Self, living in the hearts of all. He who diffuses breath with the help of Wyana is your Self, living in the hearts of all. He who goes out with the help of Udana is your Self, living in the hearts of all. Your own self lives in the hearts of all.'

Ushasta said: 'As one might point and say "this is a cow; this is a horse", explain Spirit; that Spirit which out of sight is known by sight; that Self who lives in the hearts of all.'

Yadnyawalkya said: 'Your own Self lives in the hearts of all.'

Ushasta said: 'What Self do you say lives in the hearts of all?'

Yadnyawalkya said: ' You cannot see the seer of the sight, you cannot hear the hearer of the sound, you cannot think of the thinker of the thought, you cannot know the knower of the known. Your own Self lives in the hearts of all. Nothing else matters.'

Thereupon Ushasta became silent.

Then Kahola, son of Kusheetaka said: 'Yadnyawalkya! Explain that Spirit which out of sight is known by sight; that Self who lives in the hearts of all.'

Yadnyawalkya said: 'Your own Self lives in the hearts of all.'

Kahola said: 'What Self do you say lives in the hearts of all?'

Yadnyawalkya said: 'He who is beyond hunger, thirst, delusion, sorrow, decay, death. When saints know that Self, they conquer desire for children, wealth, companions, live the life of mendicants. Desire for children is desire for wealth; desire for wealth is desire for companions; therefore let a spiritual man transcend all book-learning, and live like a child. When he transcends book-learning and childlike simplicity, let him meditate. When he transcends meditation and lack of meditation, he becomes a saint.'

'By what means?' said Kahola.

Yadnyawalkya said: 'By whatever means please him best, so long as he becomes like that. Nothing but the Self matters.' Thereupon Kahola became silent.

Then Gargee, daughter of Wachaknu, asked:

"Yadnyawalkya! Since everything in this world is woven, warp and woof, on water, please tell me, on what is water woven, warp and woof?'

Yadnyawalkya said: 'Gargee! It is woven on wind.'

'On what is wind woven, warp and woof?'

'On the sky.'

'On what is sky woven, warp and woof?'

'On the region of the celestial choir.'

'On what is the region of the celestial choir woven, warp and woof?'

'On the sun.'

'On what is the sun woven, warp and woof?'

'On the moon.'

'On what is the moon woven, warp and woof?'

'On the stars.'

'On what are the stars woven, warp and woof?'

'On the region of gods.'

'On what is the region of gods woven, warp and woof?'

'On the region of light.'

'On what is the region of light woven, warp and woof?'

'On the region of the Creator.'

'On what is the region of the Creator woven, warp and woof?'

'On the region of Spirit.'

'On what is the region of Spirit woven, warp and woof?'

Yadnyawalkya said: 'Gargee! Do not transgress the limit; or you may go crazy,' Gargee became silent.

Then Uddalaka, of the family of Aruna, said: 'Yadnyawalkya! We were staying in the province of Madra in the house of Patanjala Kapya, studying the ritual of sacrifice.

A celestial singer entered into his wife. We asked him who he was.

He said: "I am Kabandha of the family of Athar-wana."

He said: "Do you know that thread wherein this world, the next world and all beings are strung?"

"I do not know, Sir," said I.

He said: "Do you know who controls this world, the next world and all beings from within?"

"I do not know, Sir!" said I.

He said: "Who knows thread and controller, knows Spirit, knows the world, knows the gods, knows all beings, knows all knowledge, knows the Self, knows everything."

He then explained everything, hence "I know everything. If, Yadnyawalkya! you drive away these cows without knowing that thread and that controller, you will be lost."

Yadnyawalkya said: 'I know the thread, and the controller.'

Uddalaka said: 'Anybody can say that he knows, that he is wise. What do you know?'

Yadnyawalkya said: 'Life is that thread whereon this world, the next world, and all beings are strung. We say that when a man is dead his limbs are unstrung; everything is strung on life.'

Uddalaka said: 'So it is; now what of the controller within?'

Yadnyawalkya said: 'He who lives on earth, apart from earth, whom earth does not know; whose body is earth; controlling earth from within; is your own Self, the immortal, the controller.

He who lives in water, apart from water, whom water does not know; whose body is water, controlling water from within; is your own Self, the immortal, the controller.

He who lives in sky, wind, heaven, quarters, sun, moon, stars, air, darkness, light; apart from them; whom sky, wind, heaven, quarters, sun, moon, stars, air, darkness, light do not know; whose body is sky, wind, heaven, quarters, sun, moon, stars, air, darkness, light; controlling them from within; is your own Self, the immortal, the controller. Thus He lives in all gods.

He who lives in all beings, apart from them, whom no being knows; whose body is all beings; controlling all beings from within; is your own Self, the immortal, the controller. Thus he lives in all beings.

He who lives in breath, speech, eyes, ears, skin, mind, knowledge; apart from them; whom breath, speech, eyes, ears, skin, mind, knowledge do not know; whose body is breath, speech, eyes, ears, skin, mind, knowledge; controlling them from within; is your own Self, the immortal, the controller.

Thus he lives in man's body.

He who lives in man's seed; apart from it; whom man's seed does not know; whose body is seed; controlling it from within; is your own Self, the immortal, the controller.

Invisible, He sees; inaudible, He hears; unthinkable, He thinks; unknowable, He knows. None other can see, hear, think, know. He is your own Self, the immortal; the controller; nothing else matters.'

Thereupon Uddalaka became silent.

Then Gargee said: 'Revered sirs! I can ask him two questions, that if he answer, no one amongst you can defeat him in discussion about Spirit.'

The venerable Brahmans gave her permission.

Gargee said: 'Yadnyawalkya! As a soldier from Benares or Behar might string his loosened bow and rise with two deadly arrows, so I have risen to fight you. Answer my questions.'

Yadnyawalkya said: 'What are they?'

Gargee said: 'Yadnyawalkya! Tell me, on what is woven, warp and woof, that which is above heaven, below earth, containing heaven and earth; that which is past, present and future?'

Yadnyawalkya said: 'That which is above heaven, below earth, containing heaven and earthy that which is past, present and future, is woven, warp and woof, on air.'

Gargee said: 'Yadnyawalkya! I curtsy; you have solved my doubt. Now answer my second question.'

Yadnyawalkya said: 'What is that?'

Gargee said: 'Yadnyawalkya! On what is that air woven, warp and woof?'

Yadnyawalkya said: 'The saints call it the Root. It is neither big nor little, neither long nor short, neither burning like fire nor flowing like water; without shadow, without darkness, without wind, without air, without attachment; without touch, taste, sight, smell; without hearing, speaking, thinking; without breath, without face, without energy, without measure, without inside or outside; it consumes nothing; nothing consumes it.

Gargee! At the command of that Root, sun and moon do not clash; heaven and earth do not clash; moments, hours, days, nights, fortnights, months, seasons, years, follow their course; rivers issuing from the snowy mountains follow their course to east and west or where you will. At the command of that Root, people praise the generous, gods guard the sacrificer, fathers watch the sacrificial offerings.

Gargee! who without knowing this Root, meditates, sacrifices, practises austerity, though for thousands of years, does what passes away. Who dies without knowing this Root, is pitiful; who leaves this world, knowing it, is wise.

Gargee! That Root sees, though invisible} hears, though inaudible thinks, though unthinkable; knows, though unknowable.

Nothing else can see, hear, think, know. Air is woven on that Root, warp and woof.'

Gargee said: 'Revered sirs! Anybody has a right to be proud who can escape this sage, with a curtsy; no one can defeat him in discussion about Spirit.'

Thereupon Gargee became silent.

Widagdha Shakala asked: ' Yadnyawalkya! How many gods are there?'

Yadnyawalkya said: 'Three hundred and three and three thousand and three, as is mentioned in the list of the hymns to all gods.'

'Right,' said Widagdha; 'but how many in reality?'

'Thirty-three.'

'Right; but how many in reality?'

'Six.'

'Right; but how many in reality?'

'Three.'

'Right; but how many in reality?'

'Two.'

'Right; but how many in reality?'

'One and a half.'

'Right; but how many in reality?'

'One God only.'

'Then what are those three hundred and three and three thou-

sand and three?'

'The divine powers; the more important being thirty-three.'

'What are those thirty-three?'

'Eight Wasus, eleven Rudras, twelve Xdityas, Indra and Prajapati.'

'What are the Wasus?'

'Fire, earth, wind, sky, sun, moon, stars, heaven.'

'What are the eleven Rudras?'

'Five living fires, five senses and the personal Self. When they leave our body, they make us cry out; hence their name Rudra.'

'What are Adityas?'

'Twelve months of the year; they pass carrying everything; hence their name.'

'Who is Indra? Who is Prajapati?'

'Indra is thunder; Prajapati is sacrifice.'

'What is the symbol of thunder?'

'The thunderbolt.'

'What is the symbol of sacrifice?'

'The sacrificial animal.'

'What are the six gods?'

'Fire, earth, wind, air, sun, sky; all the world lives therein.'

'What are the three gods?'

'The three worlds; all the gods live therein.'

'What are the two gods?'

'Food and breath.'

'What is one and a half?'

'The wind.'

'The wind is one, why is it called one and a half?'

'Because as the wind blows, everything grows,'

'Who is the one God?'

'Life is the one God. It is that Spirit.

Yadnyawalkya said: 'Revered sirs! Anybody in this assembly can question me; I can question anybody or I can question all.'

Nobody dared question him.

Then Yadnyawalkya questioned them: 'Man is like a big tree; his hairs are leaves, his skin bark; blood can ooze from a wound like sap from a tree; there is flesh in man, wood in the tree; his muscles are like its fibres, his bones like hard wood, his marrow like its pith.

'The tree when felled grows up again from its root, from what root does man grow when cut down by death?

'Do not say that he grows from his seed, his seed dies with him; the tree can grow from its seed, its seed does not die with it.

'If the tree is pulled root and all, it will not grow again. From what root or seed does a man, cut down by death, grow again?

'He is not born again as he is; then who creates him again?'

Yadnyawalkya answered his question: 'Spirit is the root, the seed; for him who stands still and knows, the invulnerable rock. Spirit is knowledge; Spirit is joy,'

Janaka, king of Behar, descending from his throne, said: 'Yadnyawalkya! I bow. Teach me,'

Yadnyawalkya said: 'King! As one about to make a long journey is furnished with ship or carriage, so you are furnished with the sacred teachings. Though a rich king, you have learnt the Wedas and the Upanishads; where will you go, when you leave this world?'

Janaka said: 'Lord! I do not know where I shall go.'

Yadnyawalkya said: 'But I can tell you where.'

Janaka said:' Tell me.'

Yadnyawalkya said: 'In the right eye Self lives and kindles the light; in the left eye His queen. They meet in the hollow of the heart, feed on the heart's red lump, rest in the network of the veins, move through the artery that rises upward from the heart. The veins, like numberless small hairs, are rooted in the heart, through the heart flows a food finer than the food that nourishes the body.

'East, west, south, north, above, below, every quarter is filled with His breath. That Self described as "not this, not that" cannot be grasped, nor destroyed, nor captured, nor afflicted. King, he is imperishable. Do not fear.'

Janaka said: 'You have set me above fear. Here is my kingdom; here am I, at your service.'

Book VII

Yadnyawalkya went to Janaka. He had not planned a discussion; but something said about sacrifice so pleased him that he promised Janaka whatever he asked. Janaka asked permission to question him; and that was the first question he asked.

Janaka said: 'Yadnyawalkya! What is the light of man?'

Yadnyawalkya said: The sun is his light. By that light man sits, works, goes, returns,'

Janaka said: 'When the sun has set what is his light?'

Yadnyawalkya said: The moon is his light; by that light man sits, works, goes, returns,'

Janaka said: 'When sun and moon have set, what is his light?'

Yadnyawalkya said: 'Fire is his light; by that light man sits, works, goes, returns,'

Janaka said: 'When sun and moon have set, when fire is out, what is his light?'

Yadnyawalkya said: 'Speech is his light; by that light man sits, works, goes, returns. When man cannot see his own hand, he can hear what is said, and go towards the voice.'

Janaka said: 'When sun and moon have set, when fire is out, when nothing is said, what is his light?'

Yadnyawalkya said: 'Self is his light; by that light man sits, works, goes, returns.'

Janaka said: 'Who is that Self?'

Yadnyawalkya said: 'He who lives within the heart, surrounded by the senses, He is the light within, knowledge itself. Unchanged He moves through both conditions, through waking and sleeping; seems to think in the one, to sport in the other; plays amid multiform dreams, then transcends this world, transcends every perishing shape, goes to sleep.

He takes a body at birth, takes up its infirmities; but when he leaves that body, He leaves all infirmities.

He has in truth two homes, earth and heaven; but seems to have a third between, built of dreams. He stands in this third home, surveys both heaven and earth. While passing on his way to heaven, his nightly way, He knows both happiness and misery. He breaks the link. He has made dreams through his own power and light, he rejects them and goes into dreamless sleep.

In dreams he shone by his own light; no horse there, no road, no carriage, but he made it; no well, no tank, no river, but he made it; no excitement, no pleasure, no happiness, but he made it. He is the maker.

Here is my authority: "He breaks the link with all that belongs to body; he remains awake giving light; dreamless he makes dreams. By that light he returns to earth. He is the Golden God, the Man, the Self, Hamsa, the solitary Bird."

'The Golden God, the Man, the Self, Hamsa, the solitary Bird, He leaves that small nest, the body, in charge of its guardian life, goes out wherever He will, is never weary.

He the God, seems to dream, sporting among forms, to go hither and thither, seems to delight in sex, to eat and laugh with friends, or to look upon heartrending spectacles.

His playing ground is seen; no one can see Him.

Some say that dreaming and waking are the same; for what man sees while awake, he sees in his dreams. Whatever else be true, the Self shines by its own light.'

Janaka said: 'Lord! I give you a thousand crowns. Speak on for the sake of my liberation.'

Yadnyawalkya said: 'He wakes; and having enjoyed, gone hither and thither, known good and evil, he hastens back again to his dreams. But nothing can affect him, nothing can cling to Self.

Having enjoyed his dreams, gone hither and thither, known good and evil, he hastens back to wakefulness. But nothing can affect Him, nothing can cling to Self.

Having enjoyed his wakefulness, gone hither and thither, known good and evil, he hastens back again to his dreams.

As a large fish moves from one bank of a river to the other, Self moves between waking and dreaming.

But as a falcon or eagle, flying in the sky, wearies, folds its wings, falls into its nest, Self hastens into that sleep, his last resort, where he desires nothing, creates no dream.

In this body; there are those veins like numberless small hairs called Hita, full of white, blue, yellow, green, red. It is because of these that he sees himself killed, sees himself beaten down, sees himself chased by elephants, sees himself falling into a well; in all these dreams, he creates, through ignorance, dangers known when awake, or he draws upon imagination, thinking himself a king or a god or the world.

But his true nature is free from desire, free from evil, free from fear. As a man in the embrace of his beloved wife forgets everything that is without, everything that is within; so man, in the embrace of the knowing Self, forgets everything that is without, everything that is within; for there all desires are satisfied, Self his sole desire, that is no desire; man goes beyond sorrow.

Father disappears, mother disappears, world disappears, gods disappear, Wedas disappear, thief disappears, rogue disappears, ascetic disappears, monk disappears, menial disappears, good and evil disappear; he has gone beyond sorrow.

What He cannot see, He cannot see, yet He can see; sight and He are one, and He is indestructible; what can He see; there is nothing separate from Him; no second.

What He cannot smell, He cannot smell, yet He can smell; smelling and He are one, and He is indestructible; what can He smell; there is nothing separate from Him; no second.

What He cannot taste, He cannot taste, yet He can taste; taste and He are one, and He is indestructible; what can He taste; there is nothing separate from Him; no second.

What He cannot speak, He cannot speak, yet He can speak; speech and He are one, and He is indestructible; what can He speak; there is nothing separate from Him; no second.

What He cannot hear, He cannot hear, yet He can hear; hearing and He are one, and He is indestructible; what can He hear; there is nothing separate from Him; no second.

What He cannot think, He cannot think, yet He can think; thinking and He are one, and He is indestructible; what can He think; there is nothing separate from Him; no second.

What He cannot touch, He cannot touch, yet He can touch; touching and He are one, and He is indestructible; what can He touch; there is nothing separate from Him; no second.

What He cannot know, He cannot know, yet He can know; knowing and He are one, and He is indestructible; what can He know; there is nothing separate from Him; no second.

Where there is another, one sees another; smells, tastes, touches, knows, hears another, speaks to another, thinks of another.

One, without a second; that is the Kingdom of Heaven; man's highest achievement; his greatest wealth; his final goal; his utmost joy. Other creatures must live on a diminution of this joy,

When the knowing Self masters the personal self at death, the personal self groans, as a heavily laden cart groans under its burden.

When body grows weak through age or disease, the Self separates itself from the limbs, as a mango, a fig, a banyan fruit separates itself from the stalk; man hastens back to birth, goes, as before, from birth to birth.

As soldiers, governors, scholars, leaders, wait upon a returning king with food and drink and bring him to his house announcing his approach, so all the elements wait upon such a Self, announcing its approach.

As soldiers, governors, scholars, leaders, gather together to bid goodbye to a king, so when the Self decides to go, all the senses gather.'

As a caterpillar, having reached the end of a blade of grass, takes hold of another blade, then draws its body from the first, so the Self having reached the end of his body, takes hold of another body, then draws itself from the first.

And as a goldsmith takes the gold from an old piece of jewelry and shapes it into a more modern piece, so the Self forgets the old body, takes hold of another body, whether like that of the fathers, or of the celestial singers, or of the gods, or of the begetter, or of any other creature.

This Self is Spirit. He is knowledge, mind, life, sight, hearing, earth, water, wind, air, light, darkness, desire, absence of desire, anger, placability, right, wrong; He is everything; He is this and that. Whatever his conduct and character in one life, he has it in his next; if good in one, he is good in another; if a sinner in one, he is a sinner in another; his good karma makes him good, his sinful karma makes him sinful. Hence they say that soul is full of desire. He wills according to his desire; he acts according to his will; he reaps what he sows.'

Here is my authority: "'Self goes where man's mind goes. Whatever his actions in this world, he enjoys their reward in the next; that over, he returns for action's sake. I speak of a man with desire; but what is he who has no desire? He has no desire, because he has attained his desire; desire of Self is no desire. He does not die like others; he is of Spirit, he becomes Spirit."

'When all desires of the heart are gone, mortal becomes immortal, man becomes Spirit, even in this life.

As the skin of a snake is peeled off and lies dead on an ant-hill, so this body falls and lies on the ground; but the Self is bodiless, immortal, full of light; he is of Spirit, he becomes Spirit.

If man knows that he is He, why should he hunger for a body?

He, whose Self lying in this mysterious uncertain body is awakened, becomes Spirit. He becomes the maker of the world, the maker of everything. His is the world, he is the' world itself.

Let the wise and holy man know Him, govern his intellect by that knowledge} not learn words after words, a weariness to the tongue.

Holding this purpose, people long ago did not want children. Spirit was their goal; what had they to do with children? They refused children, wealth, company, travelled with a begging bowl. Desire for children is desire for wealth, desire for wealth is desire for company; what is desire but desire?'

Book VIII

Shwetaketu went to the assembly of the wise men of Panchala, and found king Prawahana Jaiwali, surrounded by courtiers. The king saw him and said: Welcome, young man!'

'Here I am, Your Majesty,' said Shwetaketu.

The king said: 'Have you been taught by your father?'

Shwetaketu said: 'Yes!'

The king said: 'Do you know if people go in different directions when they die?'

'No!'

'Do you know how they come back again to this world?'

'No!'

'Do you know why the other world is not overcrowded by those who are pouring in?'

'No!'

'Do you know when water takes the form of man and begins to speak?'

'No!'

'Do you know where to find the road that leads to God and the road that leads to the fathers? Have you not heard these words of the Sage: "I have heard of the roads by which men travel, one that leads to God, one that leads to the fathers. Everything that moves between heaven and earth, moves along these roads!'

Shwetaketu said: 'I have not heard of either road.'

Then the king offered him bed and board but the young man refused, went back to his father and said: 'Father! Why did you call me well educated?'

Father said: 'Wise man! what is the matter?'

Son said: 'That king asked me five questions, and I did not know how to answer one of them.'

Father said: 'What were they?'

Son said: 'They were these,' and told him the five questions.

Father said: 'My son! Whatever I knew, I taught you. But come, we go to the king and become his pupils.'

Son said: 'You can go alone.'

Thereupon Gautama went to the king, who gave him a seat, water and a welcome, saying: 'I will give whatever you ask.'

Gautama said: 'Say what you said to my son.'

King said: 'Why ask for a spiritual gift; why not ask a more substantial gift?'

Gautama said: 'You know well that I do not lack gold, cows, horses, servants, attendants, clothes. Do not offer me what I have already in great abundance.'

King said: 'Gautama! Then ask in the proper way.'

Gautama said: 'I come as a pupil. There was a time when people gave their word, and were accepted as pupils.'

Gautama was accepted and stayed as a pupil.

King said: 'Gautama! As your forefathers were not offended with my forefathers, do not be offended with me. I give what you have asked; for who can refuse when asked, as you have asked?

'This knowledge is not born even in a priest.

Gautama! Heaven is the sacrificial fire, sun its fuel, rays its smoke, day its flame, quarters its coal, sub-quarters its sparks. Gods offer faith as an oblation and create king moon.

Rain-cloud is the sacrificial fire, year its fuel, vapor its smoke, lightning its flame, thunderbolt its coal, thunder its spark. Gods offer king moon as an oblation and create the rain.

World is the sacrificial fire, earth its fuel, fire its smoke, night its flame, moon its coal, stars its sparks. Gods offer rain as an oblation and create food.

Man is the sacrificial fire, open mouth its fuel, breath its smoke, tongue its flame, eyes its coal, ears its sparks. Gods offer food as an oblation and create seed.

Woman is the sacrificial fire. Gods offer seed as an oblation and create man. He lives as long as he may and dies.

Then they burn him on the funeral pile. There fire is the sacrificial fire, fuel is fuel, smoke is smoke, flame is flame, coal is coal, spark is spark. Gods offer man as an oblation and create a being blazing with light.

Householders who know and worship sacrificial fire; ascetics who know it in solitude, and worship it as faith and truth; pass after death into light, from light into day, from day into the moon's brightning fortnight, from the moon's brightning fortnight into the six months when sun moves northward, from these months into the territory of gods, from the territory of gods into the sun, from the sun into lightning. The self-born Spirit finds them there and leads them to heaven. In that Kingdom of Heaven they live, never returning to earth.

But they who conquer the lesser worlds by sacrifice, austerity, alms-giving, pass into smoke, from smoke into night, from night into the six months when the sun travels southward, from these months into the world of fathers, from the world of fathers into the moon, where they become food. As priests feed on the moon, so gods feed on them. When their karma is exhausted, they return to air, from air to wind, from wind to rain, from rain into the earth where they become food, where they are offered as sacrifice to the fire in man; offered as sacrifice to the fire in woman; then they are born again. Once more they rise, once more they circle round.'

'Those who do not know any of these roads, are born as poisonous worms and insects.'

This is perfect.

That is perfect.

Perfect comes from perfect.

Take perfect from perfect; the remainder is perfect.

May peace and peace and peace be everywhere.

www.ingramcontent.com/pod-product-compliance
Lightning Source LLC
Chambersburg PA
CBHW062208080426
42734CB00010B/1835